THE TWELVE STEPS
AND THE
SACRAMENTS

"In the eight decades since their initial formulation by a handful of alcoholics with the help of a few clergymen, the Twelve Steps have aided countless numbers of women and men with various addictions overcome their unhealthy attachments and go on to lead happy, healthy, and productive lives in their homes, in society and in their places of worship. In *The Twelve Steps and the Sacraments*, Scott Weeman shares his own personal story of recovery and the stories of other recovering addicts to help us get a clear picture of the Twelve Steps and how they relate to the sacraments Christ established and left to his people for our sanctification. Whether you or someone you know is in recovery (or ought to be), whether you are a Catholic or not, this book will help you understand the sacraments in light of the Twelve Steps. More importantly, Weeman will help you see the Twelve Steps more clearly in the Light of Christ."

Marcus Grodi
Founder and president of The Coming Home Network International

"At last, a book that orients the wisdom of Twelve-Step recovery toward the grace of the sacraments and vice versa. Part memoir, part manual, Scott Weeman's *The Twelve Steps and the Sacraments* shows that the principles of the Twelve-Step movement harmonize perfectly with Catholic anthropology. It's all here: the slavery to a harmful pleasure, the realization that God alone can break the chains, the need for honest self-disclosure, and the call to help sufferers break free and stay that way. Weeman's own escape from the dark vortex of drug and alcohol addiction is proof positive that the sacraments can transform earthly sobriety into heavenly sanctity."

Patrick Coffin
Author and host of *The Patrick Coffin Show*

"*The Twelve Steps and the Sacraments* outlines in a penetrating way the essential relationship between the beauty of each step and the specific sacramental reality that can link that step to a deepening relationship with Jesus Christ."

From the foreword by **Most Rev. Robert W. McElroy**
Bishop of San Diego

THE TWELVE STEPS AND THE SACRAMENTS

A
Catholic
Journey
through
Recovery

SCOTT WEEMAN

Foreword by Most Rev. Robert W. McElroy

Ave Maria Press AVE Notre Dame, Indiana

Founded in 1865, Ave Maria Press is a ministry of the United States Province of Holy Cross.

www.avemariapress.com

Paperback: ISBN-13 978-1-59471-725-3

E-book: ISBN-13 978-1-59471-726-0

Cover image © iStock.com.

Cover and text design by Katherine Robinson.

Printed and bound in the United States of America.

Library of Congress Cataloging-in-Publication Data

Names: Weeman, Scott, author.

Title: The twelve steps and the sacraments : a Catholic journey through
    recovery / Scott Weeman.

Description: Notre Dame, IN : Ave Maria Press, 2017.

Identifiers: LCCN 2017028963 | ISBN 9781594717253 (pbk.)

Subjects: LCSH: Twelve step programs--Religious aspects--Catholic
Church. |

    Sacraments--Catholic Church. | Spiritual life--Catholic Church. |

    Christian life--Catholic authors.

Classification: LCC BV4596.T88 W44 2017 | DDC 248.8/629--dc23

LC record available at https://lccn.loc.gov/2017028963

With gratitude for their love and faith,

this book is dedicated to my parents:

Kris and Tim Rau

Jeff and Connie Weeman

CONTENTS

FOREWORD

Scott Weeman's journey to sobriety has been constantly inter-woven with the grace of God's accompaniment even when God has seemed most distant. It is this discovery that is the foundation for this book of deeply personal and incisive reflections on the relationship between the crisis of addiction and the sacramental life of the Catholic Church.

The Catholic sacraments are designed precisely to be saving acts of God that bring transforming grace to us at the most critical moments of our earthly journey. They are espe-cially relevant to the spiritual, moral, and emotional wrestling that accompanies all those who embark on the Twelve Steps toward recovery from addiction or dependency of any sort.

The Twelve Steps and the Sacraments outlines in a penetrat-ing way the essential relationship between the beauty of each step and the specific sacramental reality that can link that step to a deepening relationship with Jesus Christ. At many points in recovery, the Sacrament of Reconciliation is central, bringing with it the sense of honest inventory, humility, and a striving for healing relationships. The Eucharist remains a constant reminder to be ever conscious of God's presence, love, and power to restore us. And, as Weeman points out, even the Sacrament of Matrimony can be a deep manifes-tation of the power of letting go in the fundamental acts of grace that characterize each of the Twelve Steps in one way or another.

On one level, Weeman writes of the relationship between the human striving for recovery and the seven sacraments.

On an even deeper plane, this book of reflections, rooted in the particular experiences of various men and women facing addiction, is a testimony to the more profound meaning of sacramentality—namely, that God places tangible signs of grace and power, which can be incredibly rich sources of sustenance, all along the pathway of recovery. May God bless your journey and illumine your path through *The Twelve Steps and the Sacraments*.

Most Rev. Robert W. McElroy

Bishop of San Diego

INTRODUCTION

At the age of seventeen, I found my life changing in ways that took me a long time to comprehend. Within the space of a few weeks, I received the Sacrament of Confirmation in the Catholic Church and I took my first drink of alcohol. Little did I know how profound an effect each of these moments would have on my life. In the weeks and months that followed, I drifted further from embracing my call as a Christian as I rapidly fell into the despair that accompanied my developing alcoholism and drug addiction (or was it the other way around?). I came to know a loneliness that I once thought was impossible for a socially capable young man like me. The best phrase that I have encountered to describe the feeling of hopelessness I was sinking into is "incomprehensible demoralization." If you are struggling or have struggled with an addiction, perhaps you can relate. Nothing I did to help myself provided me with more than brief moments of peace. Any temporary tranquility I experienced was followed by a swift return to the bottle or drugs, and everything that I had worked hard for was taken from me.

What remained, however, was the one thing that I could not earn—God's loving grace and mercy. God has a tendency to work miracles near water, but it wasn't until writing this that I realized the turning point in my life occurred just steps from the salt water of Mission Bay in San Diego. After yet another moment of encountering my own hopelessness and disappointment, I pushed my bike—a one-speed, rusted beach cruiser—through the heavy sand that surrounded me. It was a gloomy day in October. Actually, it may well have been a beautiful day, as most are in San Diego, but my perception of that day, like many others, was marred by gloom. I was drinking to excess or doing drugs every day, mostly isolated and alone.

This day had started like any other. I had woken late in the morning, unable to bring myself out of bed to face the inevitably sad reality that lay ahead of me. But on this day, the pain seemed so great that I did something that I hadn't had the courage to do before. I asked for help.

Tired of the emptiness, the loneliness, and letting down everyone who cared for me, I collapsed on the beach that afternoon, exhausted by what my life had become. As the tide repeated its endless rhythm of approach and retreat, I pulled the phone out of my pocket, thinking that it had never felt so heavy.

By the grace of God I managed to call a few very close friends from back home, then my mom, and then my dad. This did not come as a complete shock to them, and I opened up to them about the darkness that had found its way into my life and my inability to do anything other than to give in to it on a regular basis. I told them that I needed help, even though I wasn't convinced I would find it.

Alcohol and drugs took everything of importance from me. They took away educational opportunities that I had worked tirelessly for. They took away career success, drove me away from friends and family members that loved me no matter what, and broke the trust that people had in me. My commitment to alcohol and drugs destroyed any chances that I had to be intimate with anyone, including God. They took away any respect and love that I had for myself and replaced them with self-centered fear and loathing that could only be held in check by more drugs and alcohol.

When I say that alcohol and drugs did this to me, what I am saying is that I did this to myself. Before I abused alcohol or became psychologically dependent on a fix of any kind, what I was looking for was some kind of fulfillment. For brief moments, I found that feeling of completion in the bottle, in the marijuana pipe, or through the rolled-up bill that I used to snort cocaine. Sometimes I would find it through the thrill of gambling with money that I couldn't afford to lose. At other times, I would achieve it by chasing women or browsing through pornography. All of the decisions I made to pursue these vices were packaged in the promise that I would be happy. They were all lies, and a mere cover-up, or attempted shortcut, to what I was really searching for: a relationship with God.

What I heard from each of those I reached out to that day was a variation of the words proclaimed from heaven when Jesus was baptized in the Jordan River: "This is my beloved Son, with whom I am well pleased" (Mt 3:17). The words used by my parents and friends differed greatly from one to the other on that autumn day, but the message was the same. I had been plunged into the depths of hell, and by the grace and mercy of our Lord, I was raised into new life.

Since that day, thanks be to the glory of God, I have not had a drink or done a drug. For someone that could not go one day without some kind of mind-altering substance, I believe that is a miracle. Each day is a blessing, and it is through the healing process of Twelve Step recovery and the sacramental life of the Catholic Church that I have the chance to lay down my head each night and thank God for another miraculous day.

My return to the Church took place within a few weeks of being granted the gift of sobriety at the age of twenty-six. To my surprise, I was not alone in experiencing a real and seemingly unending encounter with my brokenness. Those close to me in my newly found recovery fellowship and church community shared their experiences, strength, and hope with me and gave me the understanding that I was not, and am not, alone. A few of those people's stories are highlighted in the coming chapters of this book.

After about two or three months, I began to encounter the healing power of God doing for me what I could not do for myself. A radical shift—or spiritual awakening—took place within me and brought with it a commitment to turn the darkness that I once knew into my greatest asset. This shift did not take place overnight. Its foundation was laid in working the Twelve Steps of recovery[1] and immersing myself in the sacramental life of the Church.

The Twelve Steps and the Sacraments: A Catholic Journey through Recovery offers a look at the spiritual wisdom behind the Twelve Steps of recovery from a Catholic point of view. Written for both those who identify as an alcoholic or addict and those who do not but desire a fuller spiritual experience, this book will help you find a space in your own life to surrender to God's grace and mercy. It is my hope and prayer that you will be left seeking a more intimate and vital relationship with your Higher Power, Jesus Christ.

My freedom from the bondage of addiction would not be possible without the love and support that I found through the sharing of fellow recovering alcoholics and drug addicts. I am deeply indebted to all who have fostered Twelve Step recovery within the United States and around the world. These are men and women who, like the pioneers of the Church, relentlessly pursued the message of salvation and spread the Good News to all corners of the globe.

It is important for me to note that Twelve Step groups maintain no religious affiliation. However, as the wording of the steps makes clear, a constant reliance on God ("as we understand him"), a Higher Power, or a Power "greater than ourselves" is suggested (to put it lightly). These groups are seeker-sensitive, meaning that the spiritual nature of Twelve Step recovery leaves attendance open to anyone, regardless of religious beliefs. It is my opinion that this general description of God is critical to providing an entry into a spiritual way of life for people from a variety of backgrounds, some of whom come in with a great disdain for anything relating to God. With respect to this and other principles, the thoughts expressed within these pages are not related to any particular Twelve Step group or related organization.

Somewhere within the personal stories I share, I hope you are able to recognize a bit of your own story. You do not need to be an addict or a Catholic for this to happen. Even the most serene recovering addict or the most devout Catholic may find a new, personal way to understand the principles expressed in this book.

Ultimately, I have no doubt that the Holy Spirit will guide you through the process of reading, praying, and reflecting on the presence of God in your life throughout your encounter with these pages. He has worked wonders in my life, and I know he will do the same for you. The prayer and "Going Further" section at the end of each chapter will help you incorporate the wisdom of the Twelve Steps and the strength of the sacraments into your personal relationship with Christ.

The stories woven within the chapters of this book are taken from individuals who have experienced real darkness as a result of substance abuse addiction, eating disorders, mental and emotional health difficulties, sexual addiction, unhealthy relationship attachments, and other addictions, attachments, and ailments. Most of the names used in these stories have been changed for the sake of anonymity. I am full of gratitude to have the opportunity to share these stories and my own and, perhaps, give back a small portion of what has been so freely given to me as I continue to find freedom through recovery, one day at a time.

BAPTISM

1.

POWERLESS AND UNMANAGEABLE

Thomas was the kind of man that every young boy dreamed of becoming. Standing at six feet, five inches, he boasted a handsome, athletic frame and spoke with enough of a southern drawl to make anything he said seem charming. He was living his life by the rules that society dictated: be successful at everything you do, and have fun doing it. In college, he played football and won a national championship with a prominent program in the Southeastern Conference. After college, he excelled in business and was quite popular with the ladies. He had a luxurious apartment, a fancy car, a beautiful girlfriend, and a promising career. Yet, with all of this in mind and his handsome face staring back at him in the mirror, he asked himself, "Why am I so miserable?"

Sometime after college, Thomas transitioned from drinking socially to drinking alcoholically. His shift in behavior and subsequent downfall were fueled by an addiction to cocaine. Given his athletic and professional successes, Thomas seemed to be in complete control over his life and had power over everything and everyone around him. His addictions certainly did not seem like things that had control over him. Rather, drugs and alcohol were a temporary means of enjoying life a little bit more and offered an escape from a growing sense of restlessness that was creeping its way into his life.

Sure, there were consequences at times. There were some narrow escapes with death when Thomas got behind the wheel. He never showed up at his own engagement party because "one more beer" with his buddy beforehand turned into an all-night cocaine binge. Relationships with his family suffered as a result of his progressive alcohol and drug abuse, and some of the opportunities in life that seemed to have been handed to him earlier were slowly slipping away. Even brief moments of self-reflection when he questioned what was wrong in his life could not bring him to surrender. Throughout his life, Thomas had been taught that in order to succeed at something difficult, you often have to "grit your teeth and try harder." The man that got the most out of life was the one willing to go the extra mile, and he didn't need the help of anyone else. Thomas believed that one day he could be that man and manage it all well.

"For a guy with my background that came from athletics, playing football, being powerful, and having natural leadership abilities that people would follow, accepting that I was powerless was my biggest challenge. I was always taught that you never quit. You never surrender! No matter what," explained Thomas as he recalled this time in his life. "You fight until the end and then you keep fighting!"

Gradually, this stud football player who was so accustomed to winning at everything began losing more, and more, and more. Then one day Thomas picked up the phone to call his father.

After a few long rings, Thomas's father answered the phone. He began by saying, "If you are calling for any other reason than for me taking you to rehab, I am going to have to hang up." Thomas did the last thing that he ever anticipated doing: he checked himself into a three-month treatment program in New Jersey, leaving everything—including his over-inflated ego—behind.

"The only reason I called my father that day," Thomas tells me as he draws himself back in his chair while embracing the tears that slowly swell in his eyes, "was because that morning after being on a bender for three or four days—I woke up. Before that last bender I got as much cocaine and booze as I could and said, 'This is it. I'm going to kill myself. I can't live like this anymore, and I can't keep putting people through this.' I was in my apartment, by myself, snorting cocaine and drinking booze. I remember going into the bathroom and, not having prayed since high school, I asked God to please end this. I was praying to die." He was hoping he would overdose and die in his sleep, but God interpreted the end of Thomas's pain a little differently.

> After I woke up, I just knew that I was going to die on the streets. There was no other option for me. If I continued to do what I was doing, I would've died on the streets. So when I called my father, I was willing to seek help, but not because I wanted to get sober or thought that I could get sober . . . I didn't want to die on the streets. *I just didn't want to die on the streets.* Somehow, some survival instinct kicked in, but when I got to that treatment facility I had no idea I could get sober, I had no idea anything could

get me sober, and I certainly didn't believe that any human power could help get me sober.

Thomas had come face-to-face with the honesty necessary to begin Step 1: *We admitted we were powerless over (our addiction/attachment)—that our lives had become unmanageable.*

Few who find recovery do so on their very first attempt. Many of us fight our way through life with the hope that one day we may be able to manage ourselves and indulge with grace and temperance. Some addicts drive this pursuit to the extreme and end up in hospitals, institutions, prison gates, or, tragically, grave sites. Oftentimes, we try to mend relationships by proving that we can achieve short-term sobriety and that we aren't really *that* bad. We fight it. We manage it. To our peers, it seems insane. To us at the time, it makes perfect sense.

This was the case for Thomas. Mixing humor and embarrassment, he shares a scene that took place before he ultimately committed himself. He was sitting in the office of a doctor who had seen him a few years prior for a day or two of detox. They exchanged a few heated words before the doctor walked out of the room. Alone in the office, Thomas glanced at the counter where his file lay.

"I decided to take a peek at the folder," Thomas told me in a very vivid account of the moment. "Written on the folder was 'Chronic alcoholic—chances of recovery: zero.' The doctor came back in, and I chewed him out. 'What do you mean I have zero chance?' My voice boomed and I was nearly getting violent. He just looked at me and said, 'Look at your behavior right now. That's why you're never going to recover. You're filled with anger, resentment, and self-pity, and you can't stop drinking.'"

The words hit Thomas hard. He reflects back on that moment with the wisdom he has gained in working the steps:

> My problem spiritually, mentally, emotionally, and as an alcoholic is that I am powerless. If I can't accept that I am powerless, why would I seek a power? Why would I then go on to Step 2 and Step 3? Why would I clean house so that the Light can shine? Why would I do any of that? If I believe that I have the power, then I am going to manage my drinking, manage my cocaine use. I'm going to come up with the solutions, and *I* have all the answers! Or, I am completely powerless and if I don't accept that, then I have no chance to work the other steps. If I don't accept that I'm powerless on a daily basis, then there's no reason for me to seek God, and without God . . . I'm done.

Thomas made his first step.

Thomas's call for help to his father took place in 1994. As of the writing of this book, he has been sober from drugs and alcohol. Something changed within the man who once seemed to have it all. He has gone through a drastic transformation as a result of God entering his life in the most unpredictable ways. He now has a life of meaningful relationships, including a personal relationship with Jesus Christ. It is a life dedicated to serving God and others, to being a father that his own son can look up to, and to being a supportive son to his aging father as he battles Alzheimer's disease. Thomas's greatest accomplishment in life is not reflected in a championship ring, a bank statement, or the square footage of his house. His greatest accomplishment is one that he can take no credit for, because a Power greater than himself has given him new life and marked him with the seal of salvation through Baptism. Thomas's transformation has helped many others, including me, become and stay sober and has given us the chance to witness life take on new meaning. His greatest accomplishment is rediscovered time and again in the moments when he hears God whisper, "This is my beloved son, with whom I am well pleased."

Engaging the Sacrament

The plunge into baptismal waters is one that reaches the depths of our brokenness. It is said that when Christ was baptized in the Jordan River, he was submerged into hell before being raised to new life. In fact, in the Gospel of Luke, Jesus uses the term *baptism* when he talks about the spiritual plunge that he will be taking with his death: "There is a baptism with which I must be baptized, and how great is my anguish until it is accomplished!" (Lk 12:50).

An essential part of Catholic spirituality is maintaining a connection with the brokenness inherent within us. This is not a bad thing. In fact, it reminds us of our need to keep Christ—his life, passion, death, and resurrection—ever present in our lives. When we enter or exit a Catholic church, most of us make it a habit to dip our fingers into the holy water and make the Sign of the Cross. The simple plunge into these waters is a way to bind us once again with the grace of the Sacrament of Baptism, through which we recognize our powerlessness and the unmanageability of our lives, while giving thanks for the redeeming power of our Savior,

Jesus Christ. This is our identity. It is who we are, and it is who God is for us. It might seem a bit weird for someone unfamiliar with that simple ritual, but many of us seek that holy water without giving it much thought. It is part of our identity.

When I walked into a Twelve Step meeting the day after my experience on the beach of Mission Bay, it certainly felt weird as the meeting began. First, it seemed strange that the people present were mostly full of laughter and joy. I thought I might be in the wrong place. "If these people have any experience with the feelings of misery and defeat that I am going through right now, they should have no reason to even crack a smile, let alone be laughing about it," I thought to myself as I made my way to the most tucked-away corner of the room. When it came time to introduce ourselves, everyone easily announced that they were alcoholics. It was as if they were not even giving any thought to it. It was who they were. When it came time for me to do the same, it was awkward and uncomfortable. I was admitting defeat just as I perceived everyone else was, so why was my experience so different from the others? Looking back, I realize that we all had experienced the anguish of hell. However, those who held their heads high as they pronounced themselves alcoholics were bearing witness to the redeeming grace of new life that had sprung up through immersion in the healing mercy of their Higher Power—the waters of Baptism. They were not admitting defeat, but rather stating who they were in the eyes of God: beloved sons and daughters, despite their dark pasts. I began to find identity—and later, purpose—in the brokenness, powerlessness, and unmanageability that brought me there.

"You and I are going on a journey together, and neither one of us is coming back," said the man that walked
me through my first several months of recovery as his
eyes pierced through my being, seemingly giving him
access to the most hidden regions within me. He was
right. Clothed in the grace of Jesus Christ, yet viscerally
in tune with my own brokenness, I could not return to
where I had come from. Sure, I could revert back to the
old addictive behaviors, but not without that place in
my soul that had been aligned with God's mercy. The
Catechism of the Catholic Church notes that "Baptism seals
the Christian with the indelible spiritual mark (character) of his belonging to Christ."[1] A thorough Step 1 is
aimed at sealing that same indelible mark. It seals our
identity.

The first step is a crucial starting point where the
insufficiency of our human resources is brought to light.
This step is a tangible way to carve space in our lives to
surrender to the mercy made available by God's grace.
Many of us like to think that we can achieve the work
of the divine all by ourselves. Within this group, there
are a handful of people who, after a few unsuccessful
attempts, have collected enough data to determine that
the best path in life is the one paved by God's will. Others need to be mangled quite a bit before returning to
the garments of Baptism or other avenue of deep surrender. It is suggested that, during the course of working
through Step 1, we write down compromising situations
where behavior (prompted by what we like to identify
as our "addiction") has put us and others in harm's way.
It is a simple, yet hardly easy, way of coming to terms
with the darkness that our own will has propelled us
toward. Much of the wreckage of my past that I shared

in this book's introduction was uncovered in working through Step 1. I slowly began to realize how much I had put myself and others in physical danger, destroyed relationships, and stolen the peace of mind of those closest to me.

Those suffering from an addiction may know too well that one symptom of their disease is denial that they do, in fact, have a disease. Putting the work of recovery down on paper reminds us of that from which we have been delivered. "When I get to thinking that I may not actually be an alcoholic, I look back on my first-step work and think, 'I may not be an alcoholic, but whoever wrote this stuff down definitely is!'" recalls a man who has been sober for more than thirty years. There is a similar impact that humbles and unites us when we join in prayer at the beginning of Mass. While touching our brokenness and need for a savior, we proclaim:

> I confess to almighty God, and to you, my brothers and
>   sisters,
> that I have greatly sinned in my thoughts and in my
>   words,
> in what I have done and in what I have failed to do,
> through my fault, through my fault, through my most
>   grievous fault; therefore I ask blessed Mary ever-Virgin, all the angels and saints, and you, my brothers
>   and sisters, to pray for me to the Lord our God.[2]

One of the most beautiful moments of the Catholic Church's liturgical year takes place during the Easter Vigil, when new members of the Church are baptized in the name of the Father, Son, and Holy Spirit, and then all of us in the gathered community are called to renew our baptismal promises. In fact, the early Church recognized this aspect of the faith as being so critical that the season of Lent was established to allow all of the faithful to journey with the catechumens (those preparing to be baptized) as they learned to recognize and admit their inherent powerlessness. Much as Jesus came face-to-face with human vulnerability as he roamed the desert for forty days, we too are given the season of Lent to reclaim the fact that our power comes not from ourselves. The activities of the Church during Lent move us toward Baptism—either for the first time or with heartfelt and determined renewal.

As was the case when I attended my first meeting—my life a mess and everything about me awkward and in a state of confusion—there are few more powerful Twelve Step meetings than the ones where a newcomer reveals his or her situation and need for help. I can attest that this admission is accompanied by very little hope that the process of overcoming an addiction will work, but we put faith in the fact that others have gone before us and have experienced new life. In whatever fashion they admit defeat and powerlessness, each person present is given the chance to renew the vows of their own first step as they maintain the truth of their own brokenness. I can think of nothing that is more spiritually grounding for me than when I now have the chance to sit in the room at an addiction recovery meeting with people who are new to the program—people caught up in a state of hopelessness with which I am all too familiar. In many ways, what they provide the group is just as powerful as what the group can provide them. This spiritual give-and-take is at the root of recovery fellowship.

I recently had the pleasure of getting to know a woman named Maria, who was returning to her

recovery efforts and had celebrated ninety days of
sobriety from alcohol and drugs. She shared an incredible story about an incident that had happened three
months earlier. After many years of battling with the
devastation caused by her addiction, she had an alco-
hol-induced accident and fell into her swimming pool.
She was immersed in the water for up to six minutes
before her child found her nearly lifeless and called for
her husband. Maria was pulled out of the pool and given
CPR by her husband, whom she had taught the proce-
dure. After being taken away by paramedics and spending a few weeks unconscious in the hospital, she finally
returned to consciousness with a new chance at life.

I could not help but connect Maria's story of new
life born of water and saving grace to the renewal of life
offered to us by Baptism. St. Paul writes in Colossians:
"You were buried with him in baptism, in which you
were also raised with him through faith in the power
of God, who raised him from the dead. And even when
you were dead in transgressions and the uncircumcision
of your flesh, he brought you to life along with him"
(Col 2:12–13).

Listening closely to every word coming from
Maria's mouth as she detailed the miracle that God
had worked in her life, I was able to find my own story
within it. I felt buried by the depths of despair into
which I had allowed my addictive lifestyle to lead me.
I felt anything but worthy of another chance. It took a
deep plunge into the unknown before I was awakened
by a glimmer of new life. It was impressed upon me very
early that if I wanted the necessary spiritual awakening
required for a life of sobriety, I would need to ask God
for humility and honesty. I was significantly lacking in

each of those virtues, which was a reminder that, left to my own devices, I could not recover or find salvation.

✝

Let Us Pray

Lord,
I begin this process seeking an open heart
and an open mind.
Please help me shed my personal ambitions
for the sake of finding a new experience with you.
Please enable me to set aside everything I think I
know for an open mind and a new experience.
Remove any denial that may get in the way
of seeing my condition exactly as it is.
Help me to see the truth about my addictive
behavior and the parts of my life that shut out
the sunlight of the Spirit.
Offer me the opportunity to see the true meaning
of powerlessness over people, places, and things.
Just as your own baptism identified you with the
broken and made you one with sinners,
I look to the waters of Baptism
to acknowledge my broken ways
and clothe myself in your redeeming grace.
Thank you for providing me this path
to co-creating my life with you, my blessed Lord.
Amen.

Going Further

1. What fears do you have about plunging yourself into the grace that Baptism brings? What types of confusion, chaos, and/or doubt are present in your life that seem to stand in your way?

2. What parts of your life do you feel powerless over?

3. What are some aspects of your life that you find yourself fighting until the bitter end?

4. Considering that an addiction can relate to any substance, psychological dependence, healthy or unhealthy routines taken to the extreme, or continuous mental obsession, what are the addictions that keep you distant from God?

5. Make a list of roughly ten compromising situations you have personally experienced because of your addiction.

6. How has this behavior also put others in harm's way?

7. What are ten things you want out of a life that is free from this addiction? Do not hesitate to dream big here!

2.

COME TO BELIEVE

My vision of God was remarkably different when I started this journey than it is today. The shame and disappointment that had become a very real part of my day-to-day life manifested themselves in my understanding of God and the relationship I had with him. God was, in my perception, not a part of who I was but rather a distant entity that simply looked down on me and acted as some sort of divine scorekeeper. Never worthy of approaching God with the unrest I was facing, I believed that I needed to make progress on my own before sitting down at the table with him—like getting in shape before heading to the gym. Unfortunately, even my best efforts left me with a progressing drug and alcohol problem.

I know I am not alone in having had a view of God that skews away from love, mercy, and compassion. In fact, this concept of God, or a "Power greater than ourselves," is one that people new to the rooms of recovery get hung up on all the time. A variety of factors can lead to a distorted understanding of our Creator and can shape our relationship with God in a such a way as to leave us alienated from God and often fearful of or angry with him. For some, it may have been a negative experience with someone that they think of as religious. In other cases, the media's portrayal of what Christians or other people of faith stand for may have rubbed the former believer the wrong way. For yet others, it might be as simple as the boredom they experienced sitting at Mass as a child that kept them from returning to church once they were making decisions for themselves about religious participation.

These stumbling blocks to faith are more closely connected to one's relationship with the Church than with God, but the two seem to be inextricably linked. When someone begins to believe that their fellow churchgoers cannot be trusted, they tend to form the idea that the God they worship cannot be trusted either. Sadly, I regularly hear people claiming that they are "recovering Catholics," referencing the pain they have felt from their past relationship with the Church and with God. A recent statement spoken by a woman new to the process of Twelve Step recovery makes this point. "I'm having a very hard time wrapping my head around the whole God thing!" she exclaimed through the emotional pain that simply speaking about it brought forth. "When I hear the word 'God,' it makes me think of Jesus Christ. When I think of Jesus Christ, it makes me think of the house that I was raised in, which was full of chaos and confusion. I believe it's going to be a difficult barrier in this process for me to overcome," she concluded, referring to her experience with foster parents who identified as Christians but whose actions toward the children in their home were anything but Christian.

We have a tendency to view our relationship with God through the same lenses that we use to view our relationships with other human beings. During the darkest time in my life, I felt so much shame for the wrong that I was cycling through that it became clear to me that no one should trust me or unconditionally love and support me. I imagined that God was especially disappointed in my behavior as he looked down upon me from his throne while keeping a log of all the wrongs that I had done. His ledger held only negative behavior without anything leaning toward redemption. As my first few weeks of recovery unfolded, I realized that I had to recalibrate my relationship with this God.

The second step of recovery suggests that we come to believe that a Power greater than ourselves can restore us to sanity. There are a few implications here. First, this step rests upon the idea that our behavior and lifestyle are painted with insanity. The cycle of addiction, by nature, fits a definition of insanity that you are likely familiar with: doing the same thing over and over while expecting different results. A thorough first step is required before getting to Step 2. Once we come to realize that our lives are unmanageable, we can find the necessary motivation to put our lives into the hands of another. For some time, my life seemed to be a horrific *Groundhog Day*-esque repeat that illustrates the cycle of addiction and insanity. I woke up each day committed to making a change in my life that would break me free from the pitfalls of drugs and alcohol. Slightly hung over and full of the anxiety that the reality of another day brought, I told myself that this was going to be the day I got things together and stayed sober for twenty-four hours. A few hours into an unproductive day at work, some coffee, and enough hydration typically had me questioning my earlier commitment by about noon. As

I started feeling better, I would consider my resolution for sobriety a bit of an over-reaction, and the compulsion for a drink began to rule my thinking and behavior. Unable to wait until I got home, I would visit the liquor store next to work, where I typically bought a bottle of vodka and a 32-ounce Gatorade. While still in the parking lot, I chugged about half the Gatorade and diluted the remaining sports drink with vodka to take the edge off on my short commute home. Most nights ended in isolation, where I drank by myself in front of the TV and became a resentful social media voyeur of those I knew who were leading happy and productive lives. I stayed up as late as I could to put as much distance as possible between myself and the inevitable reality and responsibility that awaited me the next morning, typically drifting off in some form of a blackout before being rudely awakened by my alarm. In the morning, of course, I swore off drinking and made a flimsy decision to get my life together with the day in front of me. A few hours later, the obsession came back, and I was stuck on the merry-go-round of insanity.

Woven within this web of broken promises and disappointment were a myriad of lies and deceptions, not to mention the people I put at risk by driving while getting intoxicated. Even the two DUIs I received were not enough to awaken me to the possible consequences of my dangerous behavior. I was a slave to drugs and alcohol, and my life had become unmanageable. There was no freedom or choice at this stage of my life, as alcohol and drugs served as both the cause of my grief and the best solution, if only temporary, to the hell that I was living in. I did not believe there was a way out, and

I figured I would be living the rest of my life with this despicable handicap that had become all too familiar.

If you have had the misfortune of watching the life of an addict closely, you probably asked yourself why someone would sabotage his own life by repeatedly making the same ridiculous mistakes. I am pretty certain that this was true for those in my life who questioned why I was unable to let go of the source of my self-inflicted suffering. "Can't you just go out and have a good time while only having one or two drinks?" "You know that if you don't stop drinking and doing drugs, you're going to lose all that you have remaining in your life, not to mention any chance of regaining what you've already lost." These were just a couple of the remarks that I heard from those who cared about me and loved me. The fact of the matter is that they were right!

I repeatedly asked myself the same questions as I wondered what made me different from those who could drink normally. My self-defeating behavior around alcohol and drugs seemed insane, and to the sane person it didn't make any sense that I should keep at it. I had transitioned from the point of being able to drink socially to the place in my life where I was incapable of taking a drink or doing a drug without the obsessive response that I needed more. Unfortunately, more was never enough. Thanks to working through the Twelve Steps of recovery and offering my life to the care of God, I have been freed from the compulsion of craving the first drink or first drug. However, like a pickle that can never return to the days of being a cucumber, I will never have the capacity to drink like a gentleman again, and that's okay. My initial understanding of that reality inspired me to be open to an altogether different way of life.

A necessary component to working Step 2 is open-mindedness. The process of coming to believe that a Power greater than ourselves can restore us to sanity requires that we set aside the urge to refute that possibility, whether we are a devout believer, an atheist, or somewhere in between. To most of us who begin the road to recovery, the idea that some unseen Power can influence our lives positively seems unbelievable. By the grace of God, however, the belief does not need to come all at once. Being open enough to *come to believe* is different from believing. It is a process, and it is made easier by the aid of those who were once in our shoes and have found freedom through the aid of a Higher Power.

A gentleman named Brock was instrumental in helping me come to believe in a merciful God that truly had an interest in my life. Brock shared with me, through his own experience, that God cares about us and that divine intervention was possible in my life and could be made real if I was open to it. At this point in my recovery, I lacked a relationship with our Savior, Jesus Christ. What I did have, though, was a relationship with a young midwestern man named Brock who had a deeply personal connection with Christ that clearly shaped his whole life.

Brock is the kind of guy that wears God's love on his sleeve and passes it along with a firm handshake and a big smile. I first met Brock while attending a few young-adult Bible studies while I was active in my addiction, doing what I could to appease my Catholic girlfriend at the time. Even then, when I had little enthusiasm about anything faith related, Brock showed enough interest in getting to know me that we exchanged phone numbers and grabbed a burger together once after Bible study. As my life was spiraling out of control, that burger and the personal encounter that accompanied it offered brief relief from the anxiety my unmanageable life was creating. About eight months later, when I was at my lowest but two or three days sober, I decided to call Brock.

After we spent more time together, I realized I had to share this shameful secret that I had been hiding from Brock. I wasn't sure if he would respond to my admission of being a drug addict and alcoholic with love or condemnation, but it was worth finding out. As we were driving somewhere one Saturday morning, I suddenly just blurted it out. "Brock, I need to tell you something that's been a pretty big part of my life," I said, keeping my eyes on the road in an effort not to catch a glimpse of his reaction. "I'm in recovery from being an alcoholic and a drug addict. I'm trying to find some kind of relationship with God in order to help me through this very difficult process, and it's been made a lot easier with you by my side. I need your help." There was silence for a second as I waited for his reply, anticipating that he might want me to pull over and drop him off somewhere because he didn't feel comfortable being in the car with some guy he recently met that has a problem with drugs and alcohol.

"Wow, thanks for sharing that with me. That takes a lot of courage," he replied. "You know, there's something beautiful about those that seek God in the midst of such a difficult time." It seemed as if his words were being spoken straight from the mouth of Christ. Not only did Brock double down on his support of me, but

also he shared with me a little bit of what he was struggling with at the time. It was one of the first moments
that I experienced the power of vulnerability and honesty. I had spent years being ashamed of the truth of my
situation, hiding my reality from everyone I came into
contact with. Now I was confronted with the beautiful
notion that if I am open, weakness leads to unity, and in
unity there is victory. My attitude changed from victim
to victor with the spiritual aid of God and the help of
others.

Thomas, the stud–athlete–turned–cocaine–addict
described in the first chapter, tells a bit about how he
came face-to-face with the spiritual aid of God and
others. His story bears witness to the power of just the
slightest amount of open-mindedness. When we crack
the door open to the idea that God can restore our lives,
he responds by breaking the door off its hinges. Thomas
recalls a moment that helped fortify a true relationship
with God and overcome some of his distorted notions
of who God is.

> I always believed in God, but it was more of a judg-
> ing God: right or wrong, black or white. I had left
> him long before. I obviously believed he didn't want
> anything to do with me. Why would he? I was liv-
> ing a self-centered, self-sufficient life. There's no
> God in that lifestyle. I was lying, stealing, and cheat-
> ing to get by. However, down deep I always knew
> there was a God, and I was angry at him. I ended
> up staying a couple more months at the treatment
> place and I hated that I had to be there. I directed
> my anger at God, and they told me to talk to him
> about what I was angry about. I did, and I found I
> was mad about being an alcoholic.

Why did this happen to me? My sisters don't have it. My mom and dad don't have it. It was a self-pity form of anger. I got in a conflict with another male patient to the point where I physically wanted to harm this guy. I was so raw with emotion, and I hit my knees and was praying in my room, screaming at God! "You've got to help me! Why aren't you helping me? You say you're there but I'm ready to rip this guy's head off!" I remember I walked down to the far end of the property, far from where I was because I was trying to put space between me and this guy. I was physically going to do harm to this individual. I also knew that they were probably going to kick me out if I did do it, so that scared me too. I looked and saw Jim, the facility manager, who never leaves the main office and is never on the property. That shocked me, and I thought, "What is this guy doing here?"

After he noticed my frustration, I told him, "I am so angry and you guys keep telling me that God's listening and I'm screaming for him to help me and I'm (bleepin) falling apart here."

Thomas pauses. As he tells me this story, I see him getting lost back in that moment that took place more than two decades ago. His face makes a 90-degree turn toward me, and I can see tears rolling down his tanned face.

"Jim looked at me, and he said, 'I'm here talking to you.'" After another long pause, Thomas continued. "And that was God. As soon as he said that, all the anger left. Hard to explain. I knew that was God. The chances of us being together, Jim and I, at this point . . . the odds of that are inexplicable. There's no formula that can come up with the odds of that. But the relief I got when he said those words," he made time for one last tear, "that was a day that I really believed and started to realize that God was loving, caring, and forgiving."

Engaging the Sacrament

When Brock and I started our friendship, we encountered a number of adults who were choosing to enter the Catholic Church through the Rite of Christian Initiation of Adults (RCIA). I recall having a bit of envy as I saw others making the decision to commit themselves to God by preparing for reception of the Sacraments of Baptism, Confirmation, and Eucharist. For some reason, I regretted not making my way through these Sacraments of Initiation with more serious intentions as I was growing up. Being baptized as an infant, I didn't have much say in the matter. What helped me come to terms with my regret was that as I was working through the Twelve Steps, I was immersing myself in the sacramental life of the Church once again and had the opportunity to find God in a similar way to those who were going through RCIA. Just like those who were inspired, for whatever reason, to join the Church, I was coming to believe that a Power greater than myself could restore me to sanity through Step 2. My past provided plenty of motivation to take steps that were different from what I had tried before, giving me the openness to submit myself to a new way of life and a new Authority. God seemed to become more accessible as I met him in prayer, scripture, Bible studies, and serving those in need. Somehow, everything in my life started to connect to God.

Through Baptism we enter into the life of faith. When we approach Step 2, we find ourselves at a crossroads where we are asked to choose the path of faith in

God. It's a strong turn away from playing the director, as we have before. Opening up to the life of faith and coming to believe that a Higher Power can do anything in our lives is a big leap. So is recognizing the insanity that led us to the need for salvation. I struggled with this. It was proposed to me that I was faced with a decision. I could either continue to plod along the path that I was on, clenching the bottle and the drugs as I tried to do things my way. The experience of others suggested that this route would lead me to one of four places: jail, a hospital, an institution, or a grave. The other option was to seek spiritual help and put my faith in God. As a hard-headed individual who thought I was above any consequences, I found this a difficult decision. A thorough and complete working of the first step helped remind me of the consequences I had already experienced, and I got started on the journey while the pain of all that I had lost was still fresh in my mind and piercing my heart.

Of course, the faith that we enter into both in Baptism and through our relationship with God while working Step 2 is not perfect. Working through the steps of recovery and living a life of faith with our eyes toward heaven, we must seek progress in our faith lives and not become stifled by our lack of spiritual perfection.[1] My first sponsor, Michael, often recited two verses from St. Paul's letter to the Romans that implanted this point in my heart: "As it is written: there is no one just, not one," and "All have sinned and are deprived of the glory of God" (Rom 3:10, 23). The Church offers tools and resources to build our faith after we take the plunge into the waters of Baptism. Our parents and godparents are there for us along the way to guide us, challenge us, offer an example of a life of faith, and encourage our spiritual development. The community of believers that we enter into shares in the wonders of God's presence in our lives.

I was very hesitant to allow my church community to be a source of social, emotional, and professional support for me. Sure, I knew that I could count on my fellow believers for some of my spiritual needs, but I was happy to keep it limited to just that. In other words, I was worried about what else I would become convinced needed changing if I gave myself fully to the Church. In addition, what about all the friends that I had that didn't seem to have any relationship with the Church? My social life had never involved discussions of God, Jesus Christ, the mysteries of creation, the afterlife, or religious doctrine. If I identified all of myself as a Christian, how difficult would it be to feel accepted by others who had only known me as everything *but* Christian? Would a rapid shift in my values and priorities come off as disingenuous? These were some of the questions that I wrestled with early on, and the answers did not come until I put some action behind them.

I mentioned to some of my close friends that I was looking for help around San Diego and that I needed to start living my life without drinking and doing drugs. While these friends were a few thousand miles away in the Midwest, they were willing to be a part of my community through accountability and encouragement. That accountability developed into a two-way street, as one of my friends mentioned that he was inspired by my daily report to him and the others. As I checked in to let my friends know that I had been sober over the past twenty-four hours, he decided to make a commitment to read a chapter of the Bible each day and to send a text message with his results, using the tool of accountability to reach a spiritual goal that he had set for himself. This impulse triggered a series of conversations among some of my closest friends—most of whom I had known since second grade—about the spiritual journey that each of us was on. It was something that we largely hadn't spoken about before, and a subject that I had been afraid to open up in our conversations together.

We began reading the Bible together, about a chapter a day, which was a new endeavor for most of us. Suddenly our friendship was growing on a deeper level. We were able to pray with each other and share some of our wounds. Once a week, we joined in a virtual video chat to discuss what we had read and to analyze how the chapters of the Bible we read that week applied to what we were going through. Of the six of us that took part in this chat, only two were Catholic, but that did not stop us from sharing the Good News of Christ's salvation with each other. The Christian fellowship that formed is one of many gifts that unite us today, just as Baptism into Christ's death and resurrection unites Christians of all denominations.

Like the group of Christians I was connecting with, the individuals of the Twelve Step meetings I was attending represented a wide variety of attitudes in their relationships with God. It took me a while to realize that the God of my understanding was not necessarily the same as the God of other people's understanding. Some defined God by acronyms: Group of Drunks, Great OutDoors, Good Orderly Direction. For some, the strength of the group we met with on a regular basis was a Power greater than themselves, and that was the Higher Power that they relied on. These people were still having a difficult time admitting to the existence of a God that created the world and lives among us today. I wondered, "How can they rely on such a flimsy idea of God?" All the representations of God that I had known in my life were of God as Creator of the universe and a God who became human in Jesus Christ. Yet, in this weird transition period when I started actively engaging a faith that was planted within me from a young age, I came to realize that others were able to stay sober for a long time while relying on the group or the Twelve Steps as the Good Orderly Direction that they came to believe could restore them to sanity. I couldn't argue with their results. For myself, however, I knew there were ways that I could strengthen my unity with God and lean into God as he has revealed himself in my life—as Jesus Christ, through the sacraments of the Catholic Church.

✝

Let Us Pray

Lord,
Thank you for the moments
that have brought me to this place in my journey.
As I struggle to overcome the insanity,
which can be overwhelming,
I place my faith in you as my Higher Power.
I ask for your protection and care
as I take this step toward new life.
Great are the plans that you hold for me,
and I begin to grow in willingness
to see those plans unfold.
Perhaps there are individuals in my life
who have offered spiritual help.

There may also be those who are willing
to walk alongside me
as I fall into your merciful arms.
Let me be open to receiving help
and give me humility on the road that lies ahead.
I ask this in your name and through your son,
our Lord, Jesus Christ.
Amen.

Going Further

1. What does your relationship with God look like right now?
2. Is God someone that you rely on as a friend, or merely a divine scorekeeper somewhere in the heavens?
3. What are some of the repeated, insane behaviors that keep you from finding union with the Lord?
4. What paths are available to you to become a part of a fellowship, either in your church community or in a recovery group?
5. What is your relationship with scripture like? In what ways can you open yourself to the new possibilities of knowing God through the Bible?
6. What doors of accountability are open to you as you continue on your path toward healing and deepening your relationship with God?

3.

TURNING OUR WILL OVER TO GOD

The beginning phase of my recovery was not prompted by any great act of virtue or wise decision-making on my part. It was "the last house on the block," as I have heard many sober men and women say. Everything that our culture had taught me about success was contingent upon self-will and never giving up. Step 3 seemed so contrary to that idea that I wasn't sure what to believe. What I did know, however, was that the path I had previously paved for myself was void of any success or fulfillment. I was empty, and willing to do what others who had found an answer to our common problem suggested.

One of those people who had the kind of attitude toward life that I wanted for myself was an older woman named Dorothy. She was incredibly spunky, and although her body frame was petite and her aged skin wrinkled, she sat as a spiritual giant among her fellows who had encountered the solution to the seemingly hopeless nature of alcoholism and drug addiction. I got to know Dorothy intimately when I started seeing her at Sunday morning Mass on a regular basis. She invited me to go next door to the Lutheran church for a cup of coffee (made and maintained by a Catholic) after Mass, which became a ritual of ours for a few years. These weekly encounters often began with her probing about how my recovery process was going, looking to live vicariously through my relative youthfulness as she stirred two Splenda packets into her hot coffee. The conversations we had went in a number of different directions, touching on subjects such as the relationships that were mending between my family and me, my love life (or lack thereof), or my complaints that things in my life were not progressing at the pace that I wanted them to. She was a great conversationalist and a great listener, although she usually offered the same response to whatever it was that I had to share.

"You are not in control, Scott," Dorothy stressed to me as she shook her head while maintaining a glowing smile. Her words and expression seemed so contradictory at the time, as I wondered how lack of control could bring about any sort of graceful pathway ahead. "Our troubles are of our own making. The alcoholic is an extreme example of self-will run riot," she continued, quoting recovery literature nearly verbatim and referencing a common by-product of addiction—extreme self-centeredness. She had an incredible way of recentering my short-term concerns by focusing on the broader picture. In fact, as I was regularly bringing to her my worries about life, finances, relationships, and other things that trouble most people in early recovery, she taught me that God is a master painter that carefully places each brushstroke. I was only capable of seeing the portrait of my life from a quarter of an inch away, while God had plans for something far greater than I could see at that distance.

Troubled with the immediacy of my concerns (most of which I can no longer even recall), I started to seek God's will in my daily affairs with the larger image in mind. After Dorothy and I met for coffee dates for several months, God's will revealed itself in a cross-country road trip that she and I decided to take together. Over the span of ten days where I drove and she sat passenger, we visited parts of the country that neither of us had seen before. When we weren't appreciating national monuments such as Mount Rushmore or the expansive desert and plateaus of New Mexico, she spoke and I listened. She had a lot to share about her forty-three years of sobriety from alcohol, and I had a lot of questions with just nine months of sobriety under my belt.

Dorothy's life was a continuous response to the call of God's will. She shared that when she was a young girl raised in New Jersey during the 1930s and '40s, she looked up to and wanted to emulate the nuns that had a strong presence in the Catholic school she attended. However, she fell in love with a young man that swept her off her feet, although her marriage to him failed years later after they raised a daughter and had to bury a son just days after his birth. She found freedom from her alcoholism in 1969 and stayed sober until her death in 2014.

Dorothy was constantly working Step 3 in all of her affairs. This was most apparent to me as she continued to let me be a part of her life during her last months and days. One day, as we were enjoying each other's company over a cup of coffee on a stiff wooden bench at the Lutheran church, she broke the news of her diagnosis.

She had stage-four lung cancer that would inevitably take her life. Just as she had regularly suggested to me, she shared how she was not in control and that God's will would be done. Rather than fighting the cancer with chemotherapy and radiation, she was ready to meet her Maker when the time came and had decided to live each day to the fullest until that time. She continued to live one day at a time, showing genuine interest in my life and the lives of many others, until she passed away. Dorothy affirmed what was impressed upon me very early on—that my recovery must never be one of many things on my plate, but that it must be the plate upon which everything else in my life rests. When I approach recovery that way, I have a better chance of being willing to turn my life over to the care of God.

Several great events have come my way since my journey through recovery began, thanks in large part to the guidance that I have received from people like Dorothy. As a result, my plate has been filled with a variety of beautiful opportunities and experiences. Have I done it all perfectly? No, not even through the span of one single day. I regularly engage in a tug-of-war with my ego to surrender my will to the care of God. Oftentimes, upon streaks where everything is going my way, I begin to pat myself on the back and take credit for the good that is going on in my life. My ego inflates, which eventually has me back on my knees, having to surrender again and ask God to direct my life. I was willing to turn my problem with alcohol and drugs over to the care of God because of the misery that was created and the cycle of insanity I unmasked when working the first and second steps. Clearly, alcohol and drugs were a problem, and—by a miracle that the pages of this book cannot fully explain—God has relieved me of the obsession to drink or revert back to drug use. But what about the rest of my life? Remember, Step 3 asks that we make a decision to turn *our will and our lives* over to the care of God. What an order!

It is a tall order, and it's one that is aided by working the remaining steps. This part of the process is the gateway to finding freedom and happiness by following a suggested plan of action. It is also something that I have to commit to every day, beginning with what we call the Third Step Prayer:

> God, I offer myself to thee
> To build with me and to do with me as thou wilt.
> Relieve me of the bondage of self, that I may better do
> thy will.
> Take away my difficulties, that victory over them may
> bear witness
> to those I would help of thy power, thy love, and thy
> way of life.
> May I do thy will always.
> Amen.

The bondage of self—that is my problem! It is the thing that Dorothy pointed to as the root of all of my concerns and fears. Self-loathing, self-pity, and self-centeredness: all do a fine job of describing the addict fully immersed in his or her addictive behavior. My focus on self molded a subaddiction that was made apparent to me once I started actively seeking the will of God through the third step of recovery. I found that I was just as addicted to playing the director of my own life as I was to the substances that were delivering me to the darkness that formed my reality. My need to be in control, and the inevitable disappointment that it brought, ruled my life. I attempted to control people, places, and things. If things didn't go the way that I directed, then things were not going the right way. You can imagine the amount of deception, manipulation, and dishonesty that this attitude required on the part of someone with an active alcohol and drug addiction. At times it propelled me to some rather virtuous behavior, however. I said all the right things, went out of my way to give the perception that the real me was someone who cared more about others than myself, and I bought a lot of flowers. Tons of flowers.

Typically, the show did not go the way I intended and I, along with all others involved, was left disappointed. It is important to note that my need for control did not automatically subside when I put down the drugs and the booze. In fact, without the false sense of control that drugs and alcohol provided, I knew I would be seeking more ways to feel like I was in the driver's seat or I would have to look at life through new lenses. I had to continue peeling away the layers of the onion that had formed my way of life through the years of emotional and spiritual immaturity, and that happened through some rigorously honest emotional and spiritual housecleaning and turning to the network of fellowship and support I discovered around me.

Dr. Peter Kleponis is one of the leading Catholic voices who work to bring the Catholic faith into the recovery process for sexual addictions, including pornography.[1] As a licensed clinical therapist in Conshohocken, Pennsylvania, Dr. Kleponis has been practicing in the field for more than nineteen years. Speaking with him on the nature of sexual addiction as well as addiction recovery in general confirmed what I found through my own recovery from alcoholism and drug addiction. "Most addicts live with an incredible amount of shame," he noted.

> They think "how can anybody love me?" In fact, what I've found is that most addicts live their lives by five core beliefs. The first is that I am unworthy of being loved. I am unlovable. Second, if people really knew me, they would reject me. Third, I can't count on anyone, including God, to meet my needs. So therefore, fourth, I need to find something that I can control that will meet my needs, and thus, fifth, sex and pornography (or whatever one's addiction) is my greatest need and source of comfort. These are the thoughts that get them caught up in the vicious cycle of addiction and keep them there. There's a tremendous shame that gets perpetuated with all of this.

What Dr. Kleponis asserts about the beliefs held by those addicted to sex and pornography is true for addictions across the board: drugs, gambling, alcohol, eating, and other psychological dependencies that keep us returning to the very source of our shame.[2] He shares an integral part of the solution, which, for many, is a safe way to enter into relationship with a Power greater than themselves.

> In the community, whether the church or a Twelve Step group, is where they can begin to change these beliefs. In fact, I tell people that if they ever want to experience total, 100 percent unconditional love and acceptance, go to a Twelve Step group because it's in that group where you can share your deepest, darkest secret—the thing that you are most ashamed of—and the people there will love and accept you. From that, you can let go of the shame and begin

to change those core beliefs so that your new core beliefs are: I am lovable. If people really knew me, they could love me more. I can count on others and God to meet my needs, and God and healthy relationships are my greatest need and source of comfort.

Engaging the Sacrament

Baptism unites us as one body, incorporating us into the Church and the mission of Jesus Christ. The baptized find grace to carry out this mission in a number of ways. We are purified from our sins through the cleansing of Baptism, given new life in Christ, and invited to be coheirs and children of God (Rom 8:16–17). The Spirit that dwells in us enables us to find the will of God from within ourselves, assuming that we are willing to shed our own ambitions and follow the Spirit's guidance.

The idea of the Holy Spirit is difficult to fathom, and one that I first attempted to wrestle with from purely an academic standpoint. Seeing God as Father, Son, and Holy Spirit was hard to grasp, especially with the whimsical nature of what I imagined the Holy Spirit to be. Was the Holy Spirit some sort of divine breeze that came at times, then left without warning? It was a great mystery to me, and in many ways still is today, but I came to learn about the Spirit as a part of who I am and who we are. There is a part of us, deep within our souls and inherent within the fabric of our being, that strives for something greater. That yearning, or hunger, within us can be fed in a number of ways. It seeks to be united with others and with God, but we do not always answer that call. For a variety of reasons—hurts, brokenness, the stain of original sin—we mask that yearning with the things of this world. We believe that more wealth, honor, power, or pleasure will fill the longing within us. Those things are only beneficial to the extent that we use them to help others, which is hardly the case when caught in the cycle of addiction.

Overcoming addiction is not solely a matter of stopping the behavior that is at the root of our problems. It requires developing a new way of life that relies on the guidance and instruction of a Higher Power. The Sacrament of Baptism offers new life to those that plunge into the waters of rebirth, washing away the consequences of sin and the separation from God that results. What remains, however, is an inclination to sin again. The theological term for this phenomenon is *concupiscence*. Anyone who has endured the shackles of addiction and then opened themselves up to a new way of life is painfully familiar with the lingering tug to return to the demons that haunted them. At first, the impulse does not take much prompting to emerge. Any slight trigger that might provoke us emotionally is capable of tempting us to return to our old ways. The voices that lie to us disguise the hidden torment with justifications such as, "Just one more time," "Everyone else is doing it and seems to be getting away with it," or "What is one more bender going to hurt? You'll get back on track tomorrow." Left to our own devices, we will cave to these thoughts. But, if we stay in the middle of the pack and surround ourselves with fellowship and God's love, we will be free to resist these persuasions.

Constant reminders that we are not alone, and that things will get better, will greatly benefit us. To some extent, the addict will face those temptations the rest of his life, but the armor used to fend off those attacks will grow stronger and nearly impenetrable. It will strengthen to such an extent that it no longer makes sense to us. As the baptized, we have professed our faith in the midst of others and are welcomed into the divine mission of the Church. We are learning that our lives are taking on a greater meaning, and that to live by faith we must participate in the grace we received in Baptism. A tall order at first, yes. Others have done it, though, so why can't we? Hope is coming back, and we are starting to comprehend how God is revealing his will in our lives.

The Word of God is at our disposal and is shared with us as a tool to nourish and sustain us. As a very competitive person who was well informed about what I was up against, I found much insight and courage in one particular passage from Paul's letter to the Ephesians:

> Finally, draw your strength from the Lord and from his mighty power. Put on the armor of God so that you may be able to stand firm against the tactics of the devil. For our struggle is not with flesh and blood but with the principalities, with the powers, with the world rulers of this present darkness, with the evil spirits in the heavens. Therefore, put on the armor of God, that you may be able to resist on the evil day and, having done everything, to hold your ground. So stand fast with your loins girded in truth, clothed with righteousness as a breastplate, and your feet shod in readiness for the gospel of peace. In all circumstances, hold faith as a shield, to quench all the flaming arrows of the evil one. And take the helmet of salvation and the sword of the Spirit, which is the word of God. (Eph 6:10–17)

More was sure to be revealed, and with the gift of faith putting wind beneath my wings, I was ready to move on to a part of the Twelve Steps that I imagined would be very difficult for me to get through. United with those who were helping me along the way and brought into the life of Jesus Christ, I was at least open to giving it a try. I knew what the consequences would be if I didn't take a thorough look at what was at the root of my addiction. I had lived with the consequences of my addiction for several years prior to getting involved with recovery, and I had no interest in going back there.

✝

Let Us Pray

Lord, Creator, and author of my life,
I have made a decision to turn my will
and my life over to your care.
While that may come with fear and trepidation,
I am willing to acknowledge my need for you
as I surrender control of all that I have.
For far too long I have played the role of director,
and I am now coming to believe
that a life directed by my own self-will
is neither fulfilling nor fruitful
for the work of your kingdom.
I am open to a new way of life
that is designed by your grace and mercy.
Let me overcome my shame and fear
so that nothing may get in the way
of seeking your will.
For thine is the kingdom, the power,
and the glory forever.
Amen.

Going Further

1. What are the aspects of your life that you are most afraid to let go of?
2. What experiences do you have that lead you to believe that putting those aspects of your life in God's hands will have negative results?
3. Do you believe that you are worthy of being loved? What personal encounters have shown you unconditional love?
4. What are some of the triggers, or stimuli, that cause you to return to old behaviors and addictive cycles?
5. How can you avoid those triggers or learn to cope with them in a healthy, God-reliant way?
6. Find a comfortable and spiritually fit place to enter into prayer with God, and recite the Third Step Prayer (you may choose to do this with a loved one or a spiritual mentor):

> God, I offer myself to thee
> To build with me and to do with me as thou wilt.
> Relieve me of the bondage of self,
> that I may better do thy will.
> Take away my difficulties, that victory over them
> may bear witness to those I would help
> with thy power, thy love, and thy way of life.
> May I do thy will always.
> Amen.

RECONCILIATION

4.

FEARLESS
INVENTORY

Every aspect of my being was profoundly affected by the relief I found when I stopped abusing alcohol and drugs. My body felt rejuvenated as I stopped impairing myself on a daily basis. Emotionally, I was free from the high levels of anxiety that came when facing the truth about where my life was and how much worse it would get if I didn't do anything about it. Freed from the obsession of the mind that accompanies any form of addictive behavior, I began to challenge myself as I used to when I was growing rather than decaying. Spiritually, I was blessed with some personal encounters with Christ that fit the God-shaped hole in my heart that I had attempted to fill with alcohol, cocaine, marijuana, and other drugs.

With progress being made in each of these four aspects of my being, it was time to get honest with myself about what was at the root of the self-centered behavior that I described in the last chapter. There remained other symptoms pointing to the need of further healing. I was still prone to fear and personal insecurity. My sexual behavior was still a problem, as it was while I was in the midst of my active addiction, and reflected my need to find the same kind of short-term relief that drugs and alcohol gave me. With the encouragement of my sponsor, I began the process of digging further into who I was and what really drove my behavior. Many of the guys that I was spending significant time with repeated the saying, "You can't think yourself into right action, you need to act your way into right thinking." This was a tangible way of beginning the process of getting into action. It led me to Step 4: We made a searching and fearless moral inventory of ourselves.

Allow me to describe the specific route suggested to me in order to work through a "fearless and moral" inventory of myself. I was first asked to make a list of all the resentments that I held. That part was the easiest, because as one that was acutely aware of the wrongs done to me (at least from my perspective), I was vividly in touch with these resentments. As I began to list some of these people and institutions, I realized how that resentment fueled my behavior and thinking. Some of my closest family members and friends appeared in this first column, as well as people like my former roommate who confessed the truth of my manipulative and unfaithful behavior to my ex-girlfriend. I also listed institutions as broad as collegiate bureaucracy, which I held responsible for the difficulty I had trying to redeem my poor grades at the start of my college career and my poor performance in subsequent attempts to improve.

After specifying each resentment that I held, I was asked to thoroughly consider how my feelings toward these entities or people affected my pride, self-worth, security, finances, and personal relationships. This was eye-opening for me, as I realized that my identity was deeply influenced by the way that I was allegedly wronged by those around me. Taking it even further, I was to use the last column of my fourth-step inventory to list my part in each of these scenarios. Completing this part of the exercise was essential for me to realize the impact my personal behavior and attitude had on the resentful way of life that had became second nature to me. It diminished my identity as the victim of each of these resentments and allowed me to become both responsible and accountable to the sore spots in my heart. This process helped me understand what Dorothy meant when she said "self-will run riot." For years I had lived with these resentments, and they shaped the way that I saw the world. Comparing the final column to the first column of my inventory allowed me to see that I was personally feeding the resentments that I held while being unwilling to forgive others, God, and myself for the situations that left me the victim.

Now I am able to see how people can become just as addicted to playing the victim in a situation as they can be to drugs, alcohol, food, gambling, or pornography. I lived that reality, even in sobriety, for quite some time. Until I was willing to complete an honest inventory, I leaned toward being the victim of situations rather than being responsible for my part. Being the victim was an easy way out—I could place the blame on someone or something else. Coupled with my commitment to be the director of my life, victimhood kept me from changing my behavior. I just kept trying to keep my secrets and hide things. I honestly believed it was my roommate's fault that my relationship with my girlfriend came to a screeching halt when he told her about my behavior in relation to drugs, alcohol, and infidelity. As crazy as it sounds, I placed the blame for that relationship coming to an end on him rather than taking responsibility for the lying, cheating, and other behavior that demonstrated my commitment to drugs and alcohol over anyone I cared about. When I completed my fourth step, and then shared that inventory with my sponsor (part of the fifth step), I was able to take responsibility and be accountable for my actions. To a sane human being, this sounds completely logical. However, at this time I still had work to do to allow God to restore me to sanity.

When we take an honest look at ourselves and confront aspects of our lives that are keeping us from living in God's grace, we begin to find that our addictive behavior is but a symptom of a larger spiritual malady. St. Thomas Aquinas said that the four things we seek in place of God are power, pleasure, honor, and wealth. As our quest for each of these four things becomes more devout, the lack of fulfillment we ultimately find leaves us craving more—and more is never enough. This is what addiction is. Dr. Kleponis revealed this truth through the lens of a pornography addict when he shared his expert opinion and experience with me.

> Really, the pornography use is just a symptom. The question is, "What is the real problem here?" I think a lot of it is a search, and there is a deep emotional and spiritual loneliness. People often refer to pornography addiction as an intimacy disorder. What they are seeking is deep intimacy. Intimacy is the deep emotional connection between two people that we were created for. Ultimately, that intimacy is with God, but it also includes intimacy with each other. There are people who deep down are searching for that but may not even be aware of

it, so they're self-medicating with pornography or any other drug out there. It's said that everyone has a God-shaped hole in their heart. A lot of people do not realize it, but they're trying to fill it with all kinds of things that provide temporary relief, but there is no long-term satisfaction and they are never fulfilled.

In my own life, I self-medicated with alcohol, drugs, relationships, sexual pleasure, and the need for honor. After a searching and fearless moral inventory, that fact became much clearer to me as I saw thirty to forty pages of my resentments, fears, sexual misconduct, and insecurities laid out in front of me. Again, it was a lot to process, which is why we do not take this quest on by ourselves. God, a sponsor, and a fellowship of believers will encourage us along the way. As it was stressed to me on a daily basis, no human power could relieve me of my condition. Although science has made progress in nearly all aspects of human life, there was no pill that could cure me of the spiritual malady that the first four steps helped diagnose. The only prescription was unrelenting reliance on God, and the tools that aided me in that process were continued work through the steps, the grace that was offered through the sacramental life of the Church, and moments of mercy that broke down feelings of uselessness and an inability to forgive myself.

Engaging the Sacrament

A thorough inventory and acknowledgment of our need for a Power greater than ourselves requires awareness. When we begin to develop tools that heighten our self-awareness, we get a glimpse of the freedom that comes from realizing that our identity is not derived

from our sinful behavior. The tools that prepare us for
the Sacrament of Reconciliation invite us to get to know
the true nature of ourselves as God created us.

The fourth step is another brick in the road toward
seeing ourselves as beloved sons and daughters of God,
with whom he is well pleased. The Sacrament of Reconciliation offers the interior healing that I had been craving all my life. My perception of God began to change
into that of a deity who loved me and was waiting to
embrace me upon my return to him. Before entering
the confessional with a priest, I had to make a thorough
examination of my life up to that point. Obviously, that
included my errant ways while in the midst of my alcoholism and drug addiction, but it also enveloped much
more than that. It meant acknowledging my past while
being willing to let go of the destruction behind me.

Janice, a woman in her mid-thirties, had an especially difficult time with self-forgiveness as she found
herself battling lustful temptations, deceitfulness, and
some emotional and mental imbalances. She was transitioning from college to a professional life in her twenties
when she discovered that she was stuck in a cycle that
left her unfulfilled.

"There was a real sense of loneliness, unhappiness,
and frustration in my life," she explains in a contemplative manner, using her hands to illustrate each word.
Devoted to the expectation that she would find a lasting
sense of fulfillment through the right relationship with a
man, Janice tried a variety of methods that were fueled
by fear.

> I did not like myself. I was very much swayed and
> interested in what other people thought of me. A lot
> of my sin in college had to do with really wanting

to find someone and be affirmed by another person. I wanted to fall in love and be swept away by another person. That desire is good, and a gift from God, but I didn't go about doing that the right way. Then there was a lot of fear—fear of the future, fear of being alone, fear of being rejected. I masked a lot of that with arrogance, narcissism, and vanity.

Janice spent her time in college propelled by the fantasy that she would find happiness if she only worked hard enough for it. Good grades would mean a good, secure job down the road. That, combined with maintaining the right look and a satisfactory level of physical appeal, would make her attractive to the right man, and she would be able to settle down and find peace. However, until that time, she was driven by fear and shame. Shame came as a result of the actions that her fear drove her to. Coupled with a propensity for obsessive-compulsive behavior and high anxiety, these emotions left Janice in a very dark place and brought her to a turning point, as happens with many who struggle with addiction when a situation gets bad enough.

Her story involves a time when she was having a casual physical relationship with a man that she had known from college. As she tried to manipulate the situation so that she could benefit from both an emotional relationship with another man across the world and this physical relationship with a guy who had become her roommate, the consequences of her sexual behavior drove her into a frenzy. At one point, Janice and the man she was sexually involved with made the decision that she would use a morning-after pill. She reflects back with genuine remorse yet an honest vividness, sharing, "I started feeling bothered about our decision and looked into what the Catholic Church taught about it. It was a serious sin. It was bad. And that began what was to become a very dark plummet into serious anxiety and depression. I started feeling a lot of shame, guilt, self-hatred, and fear that I had ruined my life forever. I kept telling myself that I can't undo this, and I will always feel like this. I wanted to be dead."

The natural guilt that comes from making a bad decision or acting in a way that we know is contrary to what God intends for us can become a great gift. It is a moral compass that the Holy Spirit uses to keep us from getting too far from the life God desires for us. Janice was raised in a faithful family and committed herself to, at the very least, attending church on Sundays. "I used to go to church on Sundays when I was in college," she says, "but stopped going during this point of my life. I didn't stop believing in God, but I was not faithful and felt bad about it. Leading up to this moment of crisis, I knew that what I was doing wasn't right." Her depression and shame left her contemplating suicide until she turned to God.

Janice considered that a life of faith might be her last hope before giving in to thoughts of death. Realizing that acting out sexually was merely a symptom of some larger spiritual condition, she began looking introspectively at what was driving this behavior. In addition, she had to face the reality that she shares with 40 million other American adults—that she suffers from an anxiety disorder. "It's a part of my story and a part of my experience," Janice can now proclaim, having come to accept her condition and to be accountable for her behavior.

A focus on our sinfulness need not be taken over by morbid self-reflection. Rather, it is an act that allows us to peel away the layers of our self-will so that we may build an armor made of God's grace. Janice learned to seek forgiveness for the actions that brought her guilt. She emphasizes the importance of the Sacrament of Reconciliation in the years of transitioning into recovery and her reliance on the sacrament today. First, she had to prepare herself by taking an honest look at both her strengths and her weaknesses, and then find the necessary motivation to bring her failures to the Lord through the Sacrament of Reconciliation. Before making this transition, she explains, "I was unwilling to acknowledge that I had these flawed tendencies and was not even close to sharing them with God and with other people. I didn't ask myself any of those questions, nor did I do anything to further my self-discovery." Until one day she did.

> I began to do a lot of scripture reading. I was desperate, and willing to take an approach based on faith. I began some personal journal writing, and contemplated confession. At first I was doing it all by myself. I started a new relationship with a man that was an agnostic, and I didn't let him into any of this stuff. It wasn't until I got involved in community and started the process of getting to the root of my self-loathing, fear, and anxiety that I was able to make progress. I began to be honest with myself about the realization that I have a tendency toward obsessive-compulsive behavior and anxiety, and I wasn't able to change that.

Whether it's undertaking a searching and fearless moral inventory of ourselves, or preparing for the

Sacrament of Reconciliation by facing the truth about our behavior, if we stop there we are missing out on the grace that comes with forgiveness. If the pornography addict comes to the realization that he is filling himself with shallow forms of intimacy but fails to take the next step toward a solution, he will be left with only shame and remorse for who he has become. If I had stopped working the steps after the fourth, and only carried with me an awareness of the moral detours I have taken in my life and an acknowledgment of all my fears, I would have surely returned to drugs and booze in order to cope. Janice did not stop after coming to realize that her mental and emotional condition played a big part in her story. Instead, she plowed on to further uncover the source of her pain and the route that her life had gone. She made the difficult decision that her life was something worth fighting for, and that she couldn't do it alone. One who struggles with finding forgiveness for herself will have a hard time manufacturing it alone. God's mercy and a personal encounter with the face of Christ lie ahead, and the reward is priceless.

†

Let Us Pray

God,
I am now at a point where I am willing to take
a thorough and fearless look at myself.
While abandoning old ways and ready
for new behaviors and attitudes,
I recognize the importance of being honest
with myself and with you.
Please continue to grant me grace
to overcome any obstacles or distractions

that keep me from completely recognizing
my part in my resentments.
May the fears that I hold
and any other continued misconduct
that has directed my life
be brought to the surface
as I prepare an inventory.
I abandon my trust to you
as I complete this spiritual work,
and give all glory to you
for the freedom that may come as a result.
Your grace is enough.
Amen.

Going Further

1. What resentments do you carry? Make a thorough list.
2. How do these affect your: Ego? Self-worth? Pride? Personal security? Financial security? Relationships?
3. What is your part in each of these resentments?
4. What fears exist in your life and how do they affect you?
5. What is your part in the fear that you carry?
6. Is there any sexual conduct that ought to be accounted for, straining your relationship with yourself, God, and others?
7. How have your God-given natural instincts and desires gone too far, causing you problems in your relationship with God, yourself, and others?
8. Make a list of your personal assets. What gifts has God given you to use toward the greater good, helping serve him and others?

5.

ADMITTING OUR WRONGS

A life of faith inevitably requires regular encounters with paradox. This is especially true during the first few stages of turning one's life over. It seemed to me that everything I was asked to do in order to get sober and stay sober contradicted my previously held beliefs about how life ought to be lived. Few examples of this ring truer than my experience with Step 5: "Admitted to God, to ourselves, and to another human being the exact nature of our wrongs." I was conditioned to isolate in my weaknesses and present only my strengths to others, especially those that I was just beginning to get to know. That is the way you advance in business, it is the way you attract someone of the opposite sex, and it is the way that you prove worthy of anything you want. At least that is what our culture tells us. Now I was being asked to share my shortcomings and my entirely imperfect past with another person, and it was something that I was unaccustomed to.

When I was living in the midst of my active addiction, I was doing everything I could to give the impression that I had my life under control. I was certain that even those close to me—parents, girlfriends, siblings, close friends—would be ashamed and possibly abandon me (one of the top fears I identified as I completed my fourth step) if they knew what my life really looked like. It was difficult for me to get through the painstakingly honest nature of the inventory, but by working Steps 1 and 2, I came to realize that the path I was paving for myself wasn't working out. At Step 3, I made a decision to be open-minded about what would be asked of me, inviting God's will into the process. The first part of fulfilling God's will was completing my fourth step, which, void of the fifth, left me a bit unsettled. It was time to further the action on the inventory that I had taken and share it with God and another human being.

I had no doubt that God was aware of the exact nature of my wrongs. My impression of God as an all-knowing scorekeeper was still part of my relationship with him, although I was starting to realize that he was willing to even the score if I became repentant. However, the question remained: if God knows all of my sins, why do I have to share them with another human being? It was a question that I didn't sit with too long, as I had left behind—to the best of my ability—the impulse to argue everything with everyone. Furthermore, my sponsor had proven trustworthy, so when he stressed the importance of working the fifth step as soon as I finished the fourth, I was willing to believe in the serenity he promised I would find.

There is a significant overlap between the Sacrament of Reconciliation, specifically the confession aspect of it, and the fifth step of recovery. As it was presented to me, we can choose to do our fifth step with an individual who has had similar experiences. This may be our sponsor, or it can be a trusted individual from a Twelve Step fellowship or church community, but it must be someone that we feel comfortable being completely honest with. Often for Catholics this person is a priest, and it is completely acceptable to do your fifth step in a confessional (an appointment is suggested, because a fifth-step confession will likely be longer than a typical confession heard on a Saturday afternoon). Most priests are familiar with this process, and it is recommended that you give your confessor a heads-up prior to your meeting. I chose to do both—complete my fifth step with my sponsor (who already knew quite a bit about my situation) and make an appointment with a priest in whom I was able to encounter Christ and from whom I could receive the grace of a sacramental confession made with a contrite heart.

I was still keeping a lot of things in my life in isolation, even as I began the process of recovery. I had some secrets that I wasn't very proud of. I had a tendency to round off the edges of the truth as I shared what I was going through. Some of my behavior revolved around getting back things I had lost—such as my relationship with my former girlfriend—and could be categorized as manipulative and deceitful. I was unwilling to be fully honest with anyone about this behavior even as I was pushing drugs and alcohol out of my life. These were the things I addressed with my sponsor as we sat down together and reconciled my fifth step. Had I done this alone—claimed to share my already-known wrongs with God by acknowledging them in my head—I would not have reached the depth of my troubled actions as I did when I was face-to-face with a trusted individual. I went through the inventory that I had put together in the previous step, sharing with him the resentments I held and how they affected my personal security, and concluded with taking responsibility for my part in each scenario. There were things my sponsor brought to my attention that I did not realize myself as I was putting my inventory on paper. Working the fifth step with him helped me name things that I was holding on to and perhaps subconsciously keeping even from myself.

Discussing the fears that I had journaled about helped me see how my behavior was shaped by those fears. My sponsor helped me trace my fear of abandonment to episodes in my childhood and experiences I had as I was growing up. I was amazed to see how some of my adult relationships, not just romantic in nature, had been undermined by the underlying fears that I brought into them. Shockingly, as we discussed these experiences, I felt more and more at peace to have finally been able to share some of these things with another individual who was not there to make judgment, but simply to help me process my experiences.

Throughout the hour or two that we spent together combing through my inventory, my sponsor offered objective insight into the nature of who I was and what I had gone through. He also wove some of his own shortcomings into this grace-filled time, thus putting me at ease, helping me know that I was not alone and that someone whom I had developed a great deal of respect for was not entirely perfect. We finally made it through the dreaded sex inventory, which I packed a lot of shame into. Paradoxically, as I shared the shame that filled my heart because of my sexual behavior, I felt free of the power it had held over me—something I hadn't fully realized until then.

Some of the most profound experiences that people have shared with me about working through the Twelve Steps have involved Step 5. One man named Gerald detailed the healing nature of sharing his inventory with a priest. Through much of his life, Gerald had been weighed down by habits of sexual deviance. At first it was something he believed was not that big of a deal, rationalizing that all men act out through masturbation and various methods used to heighten the experience. He had started masturbating in his teenage years, and had spent so much of his life partaking in it that it became as regular an experience for him as brushing his teeth or taking a shower. "All guys do it, it's part of our biology," we may think to ourselves to justify this selfish behavior while not knowing any better. What started with a few magazines hidden from Gerald's parents soon became an addiction without him even recognizing it.

Gerald had been sober from alcohol and drugs for more than fifteen years when he came to the realization that the common thread in his failed relationships was him. While he could point to outside reasons why each of his two marriages did not work out, the real pain of pornography use had impacted a recent romantic relationship, leaving him with an all-new awareness of his powerlessness. He had worked through the Twelve Steps of recovery several times while maintaining his sobriety, recognizing the need for spiritual help with his addiction to drugs and alcohol. However, during those times, pornography had never surfaced as an issue he needed to face in order to strengthen his relationship with God and others. Once Gerald experienced enough pain, together with a moment of humiliation, he made a decision to do something about this addiction.[1]

For a while, Gerald supplemented his Twelve Step fellowship meetings with meetings for those overcoming sexual addiction. He found that the process was the same as the one he went through to receive healing from his alcoholism and drug addiction. He was willing to go to any length, which included using accountability software on his computers, phone, and tablet.[2] An accountability partner received weekly reports that detailed any online behavior that resembled inappropriate content. After completing his fourth-step inventory on this issue, noting his resentments, insecurities, and fears that were wrapped in acting out sexually, he was ready to complete a fifth step. Gerald made an appointment with a Catholic priest at a local parish to get honest with the exact nature of his wrongs with God and another human being.

Although he had experienced what he viewed as a miracle in God freeing him of his alcohol and drug problem (one day at a time), Gerald still held a bit of disbelief that the compulsion to masturbate and look at pornography could be lifted. After all, this behavior had been ingrained in him for more than three-quarters of his life! He entered the face-to-face meeting with the priest with some hesitation, but the results he found were shocking. He was relieved of the mental obsession to view pornography and was granted opportunities to practice patience in the process. After reaching the turning point of surrender, Gerald became open to what God had in store for him. By God's grace, that meant a happy relationship and moments to be a positive example to his son.

Engaging the Sacrament

If there is a common thread in the stories that I have shared thus far in this book, it is that we cannot do this alone. It is in isolation that we fall back into the tendencies that brought us to our knees in the first place, and rigorous honesty with ourselves, with God, and with others is paramount. Janice learned this progressively as she leaned into the truth that surrounds the beauty of sacramental grace. Confession was, and still is, a big part of what brought her closer to God through the process of overcoming her self-seeking fears. After living through a dark period of depression that had her questioning everything in her life, she felt compelled to seek the truth about herself and the merciful nature of God by getting involved in community.

My experience was very similar to that of Janice. Brock and other young men who were willing to listen to me and share moments of delight and despair, all while encouraging my progress, helped me get to know myself in a way that was more aligned with who God saw me to be. I experienced precious moments when I felt cradled by God the Father and the people that he put in my life to lift me when I couldn't lift myself. A lot of those moments occurred when I was spending time with my sponsor, Thomas, who helped me feel safe. He, of course, had his own experience, strength, and hope to share with me as he highlighted how others impacted his transition into a fellowship and new way of life. "I learned that when I collaborate, things usually come out better when it is a participatory process rather than 'my way or the highway.' A guy named John [whose story I will share in the concluding chapter of this book] used to tell me to be open and get as much information as possible. As long as I am open and participating in the fellowship, that is where the peace and relief from fear would come. I'm now a part of the herd. I'm not trying to run the herd, and I'm no longer outside of the herd. I'm a *part* of the herd."

The Sacrament of Reconciliation is a very personal one-on-one experience with the face of Christ. At the same time, it is a pull away from the isolation that we can find ourselves living in. It is an invitation to be a part of the herd. This invitation is one that is always available and can be accessed at any time. Granted, it is an invitation that can seem daunting to someone that has been away from the sacrament for quite some time. I know this because for a long time, I was in a place where I felt as though no one could help me. I was trapped, had a very fragile ego, and felt that I could not trust anyone.

Having been given daily access to a new way of life, I can now see that the devil arranges our shame to keep us isolated and seeking, more and more, the source of our shame. For me, it was alcohol and drugs. For some it is the comfort of a slot machine, the obsession to find the right relationship, or the momentary hit of serotonin (the brain chemical that produces the "feel good" effect) that comes with pornography and masturbation. I was so afraid to ask for help, and it wasn't until the pain overwhelmed my fear that I sought community. It was through the loving presence of fellowship that I was moved to seek the Sacrament of Reconciliation, which of course includes confession to another person, a priest.

"This is where that change occurs and it is so important," remarks Dr. Peter Kleponis. "I get so frustrated when I hear people say, 'I'll do it by myself, I'll read a bunch of self-help books, maybe I will see a therapist, or I will do some online program.' They don't succeed because they are allowing their shame to rule their lives, and being part of a community requires giving up some of that shame. Also, they're not getting the benefit of being in that loving community." Emphasizing use of the sacraments of the Church to accompany one's addiction recovery, Dr. Kleponis stresses the importance of Reconciliation. "With the Sacrament of Reconciliation, a man goes to a priest and he encounters in that priest Christ, who says, 'You are not only forgiven, but you are reconciled.' Things are right between us now, and I love you. This is one way of letting go of a lot of the shame and being reconciled. There's so much healing that comes along with this."

Gerald, who found it necessary to analyze the role of pornography and masturbation in his life after twenty years of sobriety from alcohol and drugs, experienced tangible reconciliation through working the fifth step and bringing a willingness to change into confession with a priest. "When I did that fifth step last summer with that priest, there was no doubt that God was in that room," Gerald shares, his demeanor holding the pain he brought into that encounter and the freedom he left with. "There is no doubt that I was kneeling in front of the Blessed Virgin Mary. Kneeling, praying, and crying. There was no one else there. Something . . . ," he paused for a moment while fighting back tears, ". . . touched me on the shoulder. It was God."

✝

Let Us Pray

Father,
Forgive me, for I have sinned.
Inspired by the fearless and searching
moral inventory that I have put forth,
I seek you for forgiveness and guidance.
Open my heart and mind to the graces of
Reconciliation
and let me be willing to come to you
as my protector and light.
Let me not fear the rejection
that may hinder coming to you,
but rather let me lean into your divine mercy
and grace
so that I may provide the same to others.
Thank you for the Sacrament of Reconciliation
and for the communities that continue to direct
me toward you.
Amen.

Going Further

1. Is there anything that keeps you remaining in isolation?
2. What secrets are you holding on to that you are unwilling to share with anyone?
3. Identify an individual—preferably of the same sex and someone that is familiar with this process—that you can ask to share your fifth step.
4. Once you have identified an individual, do not hesitate to ask him or her to set a date and time where you can meet to share your inventory.

6.

REMOVING
DEFECTS

Having come to this point on our journey, we often have
been given access to a miracle we never expected—freedom from the shackles of our addiction as we used to
know it. This is not always the case, so don't feel as
though you are doing something wrong if the obsession to get your fix from your drug of choice does not
subside by this time. When we started, we had one
vision in mind (I want to say one *hope* in mind, but don't
want to diminish the weight of the hopelessness with
which many begin this journey). Our vision was, and
is, removal of our addictive behaviors from our lives.
In my case, it was the abuse of alcohol and drugs. In
Gerald's case, it began with alcohol and drugs and then
revealed itself through a pornography addiction. Janice
simply wanted to overcome her depression and anxiety. Each road to recovery brought so much more than
just freedom from the jaws of addiction. The promise
that Michael made to me at the very start was revealing
itself through a complete transformation of who I was.
His words, "You and I are going on a journey together,

and neither one of us is coming back," began to ring true through the radical changes that were taking place within me (and, as he reported, within him as well).

Since beginning this process, we have come to realize that our problems are woven into every aspect of our lives, and are not simply found in our various addictive behaviors. Remember, those behaviors are but a symptom of a larger spiritual unrest that manifests itself in an emptiness that cannot be filled. Some people find the relief that they are looking for and stop at this point. Removing the source of the most glaring hang-ups and the driver of their road to rock bottom makes life more manageable, and their willingness to complete the rest of the steps fades. I see it quite often, and those people usually return to the addictive patterns that brought them to their knees. This is really sad because they are missing out on the spiritual awakening that is promised by going through the entirety of a Twelve Step program.

A full-fledged removal of all our defects of character, known in Christian terms as sins, is a tall order. In fact, it's an impossible order of perfection that we will never achieve in this lifetime. That does not mean it is not worth striving for and holding as our ideal. Some may ask, "If you remove all defects of character, then what of my character will remain?" In other instances, we may feel that we have to rely on certain levels of sinfulness in order to get by in some of our dealings. The salesman that relies on clouding the truth in order to make a deal feels that deception and dishonesty are a necessary (and widely accepted) part of his trade. The group of friends that get together for lunch every week might be tempted to think that if they don't gossip, there may not be much to talk about. Having made a firm commitment to rely on God, surrender to his will for us, and seek fellowship to encourage us along the way, we are propelled to yet another leap of faith.

My experience with Step 6, becoming entirely ready to have God remove all these defects of character, has been painted with both success and struggle. So much changed over the course of my first two years of recovery as I started to discover who I really was, sifting through what was true about myself and what was not. My new way of life brought opportunities to take on new habits and to set new standards for myself. For years, I had lowered my standards to meet my behavior. Now I was given the strength and hope to raise my behavior to meet new standards that I was setting for myself. It did not come all at once, and if I told you that I have everything figured out now, I would be resorting to old dishonest behavior (and it would be too arduous to make amends to each person who is reading this book).

A few glaring changes come to mind as I recall becoming ready to have God remove my defects of character. The first was a battle against pride, which seemed to reveal itself in backwards ways. I was ashamed of not having completed my bachelor's degree and sometimes had a hard time accepting where I was professionally. I worked serving tables at a restaurant for three years prior to getting sober and throughout the first five years of my sobriety. It was a job I loved doing, and it paid me well while offering flexibility to do the things I needed to do to get sober and become an active member of my church parish. I worked with great people, learned skills that will help me throughout the rest of my life, and will always be fond of the times that I got to provide memorable dining experiences to guests of all kinds.

Despite all that, I never liked it when people asked me, "What do you do?" In fact, at times I responded with something like, "I play golf, I go to church, I spend time with friends, and I cook," when clearly I knew that they were asking about my profession. Without realizing it, I projected my own insecurity about my work status on the person asking the question, even though they were simply engaging in standard small talk. I would assume that the person asking was judging me or placing too much emphasis on a job title as a basis of identity. "Everyone who asks me that question is egotistical and lets their pride get in the way of true personal value," I would tell myself as I added resentments to the satchel that was weighing me down. After I spent some time contemplating what this all meant and why it bothered me so much, my sponsor helped me grasp the spiritual principle of mirroring. That is, the things that I see as bothersome in others are actually things that need to be worked on within myself. It was humbling to realize that it was my pride and ego that needed deflating. I came to understand that I was deeply insecure and was placing too much human value on a job title as a standard for one's place in life. This conception of worth contributed to my own lack of self-worth, and as I realized this, I became ready to allow God into this part of me. Coming to understand that I had an unhealthy attachment to honor, and in some ways wealth, told me I had much more room to grow and required further willingness to let it go.

A second area of my life that needed radical change was the nature of my relationships with women. Working through Step 6 on this issue was not something I eagerly approached. Thankfully, the first five steps prepared me for this part of the journey. Before I was given the gift of sobriety, I had a desperate need to be validated by the love and admiration of a woman. Much like what Janice had experienced, the longing for this connection was in fact a desire for God, a spark of divine life within me. I now see that I was replacing the natural urge to seek God's love and mercy with attachment to another human being. This mangled itself into several forms of lustful, self-seeking action on my part. Although I would, at times, act virtuously to gain the esteem of women, my intentions behind my actions were self-absorbed. Desiring to achieve pleasure and self-worth from the embrace of a woman drove me to do some hurtful things. This was made clear through a thorough fourth-step inventory, and I was given some clarity around the issue when I completed my fifth step with my sponsor.

Brock, the man who helped transition me into a sacramental life in the Church, was encouraging me to learn a new way of life rooted in beauty, truth, and goodness. I was open and willing to adopt this new lifestyle based on the teachings of the gospels and other scriptural truths I was learning. However, I had a hard time letting go of what I thought was essential to my happiness and well-being in a romantic relationship. I blurred lines around both physical and emotional chastity. I felt powerless before the temptation to sacrifice the newly found principles laid at my feet in order to appease my sexual desires. I was making improvements over my former way of life, but my conscience was at odds with my behavior and more had to be done.

I should acknowledge that one of my initial motivations for getting sober and even participating in the life of the Church was that I thought they would help me regain the woman I was dating for several years while my life was spiraling out of control. In the midst of my interior chaos at the time, I made this woman and my relationship with her my idols. I was convinced that the relationship was the only thing that could save me, and I felt that without it my life would be unfulfilled. My girlfriend had a relationship with God that I did not have, and I felt that my inroad to a better way of life would come through her. My pursuit of alcohol and drugs ultimately beat out my need to be the kind of man deserving of this woman's love. On a few occasions I heard her speak these words to me: "You must love alcohol and drugs more than you love me." While heart-wrenching to hear, this statement was true, and my actions proved it. In order to protect my addiction, I regularly lied to, deceived, and emotionally hurt this woman. After a few years of an on-and-off relationship, she had had enough of me. She needed to achieve some peace of mind, and having me around was only getting in the way of her dreams and goals.

Still, I had hope that if I did the right things, I could win her back. I was gaining new insights about myself, including the truth that self-worth and peace come from refocusing my pursuit on the love of God. It took about a year or so to overcome the idea that my life would not be worth living if I didn't resume a relationship with her. Even when I found sobriety, old habits were still in place that shaped the way I approached her and other women. Those habits can mostly be described as not staying true to who I was and what I was learning to be right. Even as I began dating other women, I entered relationships with the willingness to do and say whatever I thought was necessary to gain a woman's approval. I was turning my back on what I knew would bring long-term peace and satisfaction for the short-term rewards that left me and others puzzled.[1] Being honest with those that surrounded me, held me accountable, and encouraged me no matter what was a crucial part of recognizing my wrongs and recalibrating my behavior ever so slightly toward what was in line with God's plan for me. I slowly came to realize that in order to find the woman that I could have a genuine, lasting relationship with, I had to form within myself the character traits that I was seeking in another person. My sponsor suggested that I make a list of the characteristics I was looking for in a romantic partner. I wrote down what was important to me: faithfulness, passion, a loving nature, emotional maturity, trustworthiness, a responsible attitude, and safety in communicating with. Next, the tables were turned as my sponsor noted that if I wanted to find someone with these attributes, first I had to genuinely strive for them myself. I could no longer rely on the saving grace of a woman to transform me into the man that I wanted to be. While I was making strides in these areas already, this exercise put into perspective how I was maintaining my everyday conduct and striving to be a man of God.

Engaging the Sacrament

Several things had worked against my past attempts to get sober from drugs and alcohol. I was very young, I couldn't imagine a life free from alcohol and drugs being at all meaningful or fulfilling, and I really struggled with what I wanted my future to look like. Sometimes

I would stumble on the vision I had for particular moments in my life and not be able to get through those scenes without a drink. One specific scene I imagined was having a champagne toast on my wedding night. "If I quit drinking now, what am I going to do when that night comes? Isn't it a necessity to toast with a glass of champagne on my wedding night?" I would ask myself. With such illogical thinking, I rationalized my continued relationship with alcohol, which was contributing to the destruction of my life. I was getting way too far ahead of myself—looking far into the future while ignoring the present—and there was also deep irony to the specific idea of toasting with champagne on my wedding night. As a result of my addictive behavior (and the other defects of character that accompanied it), I was far from marriage material.

While a discussion of the Sacrament of Marriage is appropriate here, I must first share how the gradual comprehension of the Twelve Steps of recovery, specifically the principles practiced in Step 6, has helped me realize love in a new and remarkable way. Upon completing and discussing the list of character traits that I was looking for in a woman, I came to find that I was already making some genuine strides in my own behavior and relationship with God. It wasn't perfection, of course, but it was progress that I could sleep on at night. God had been carefully painting the mural of my life, and I was finally setting down my own paintbrush in order to step back and appreciate his work. I was pleasantly excited to begin courting a woman that I met in a Catholic young adult beach volleyball league and who I was getting to know as we attended the same Bible study.

There was one particular day that I recall unmistakably seeing the presence of God in her. We were transitioning our relationship from friendly to romantic, and we were both enjoying the somewhat difficult process of sharing some of our insecurities with each other. As mentioned earlier, a lot of the insecurities that I brought to relationships stemmed from the failures of my past. It was a beautiful autumn afternoon in San Diego, and we spent time praying together, getting coffee, and locating a little bench near La Jolla Cove, where we sat and watched the waves crash as we shared a bit more with each other. I had received another rejection letter from a local university that I had hoped to attend, and this was on my mind. I had completed my fifth semester at a nearby community college and was struggling to get into a four-year university to earn my bachelor's degree, weighed down by years of poor grades in previous attempts. I still had feelings that my worth as a man was defined just as much by accomplishments as by character and faithfulness.

Some tourists passed by as the topic of my education and professional goals came up. I sat in my shame for a second before letting Jacqueline know that I was trying to complete my bachelor's degree but had recently received another disappointment in the process. Waiting for her to pull away a bit, I was put at ease when I was instead showered with charity. She made it clear that what attracted her to me was not outlined by success, but by my willingness to rely on God as the author of my life. She assured me that regardless of how things worked out in that aspect of my life, she was interested in pursuing a relationship with me. She was grateful for my relentless honesty with her through matters that were joyful and painful. It was the same thing that I was hearing God say to me when I found quiet time in prayer with him. Just as I found mercy through support from Brock and countless others along my journey, here was another person that became the face of Christ for me when my feelings about myself were tempting me to feel unworthy.

We dated for about eight months, sharing more of our lives and the love that God had for us with each other, before I asked her to consider marrying me. It wasn't too painstaking of a process to discern God's will for us, as our time together was full of God's presence. I have been gifted by a tangible, vital relationship with God through the process of recovering from my alcoholism and drug addiction. Each turn brought new aspects to the God that I was beginning to understand, and my relationship with Jacqueline was another unique expression of his love. We were each making strides in our appreciation of the blessings that God had given us, and this was coming together through a union that only God could have conjured.

The idea that man and woman are created in the image and likeness of God was something I had been hearing for quite some time. Now, through the developing union with Jacqueline and her faithful approach to God's love and my love, I was seeing God's love for me expressed in the woman I was committing the rest of my life to. I saw God in Jacqueline. Unlike my previous serious relationship, however, I did not put the impossible burden on her to be my god and savior. I now had a relationship with God that I was participating in, and my marriage was another outward sign of his love and fidelity for me.

We made our marriage vows to each other in front of our families and close friends in September 2016, just a few weeks before I celebrated five years of continuous sobriety from alcohol and drugs. I was able to celebrate that day without the need for a champagne toast to make it any better. It was a celebration of the beautiful mercy that God has for each of us, and of the spousal love that Christ has for the Church. From this love stems the grace available to us within the sacramental life of the Church, as well as his continued pursuit of us as beloved daughters and sons of God. Just as the indelible mark placed upon us at Baptism can never be rescinded, the nuptial covenant that God, Jacqueline, and I entered into that day shall never be revoked.

Of course, we are in constant need of the grace that God offers us through the Sacrament of Marriage. The sacrifice that Christ made for the redemption of all and the establishment of his Church lays the foundation for this sacramental grace. That does not mean that all of my character shortcomings vanished the day I entered into marriage, just as the defects of character that I ask God to remove do not reappear when I revert back to some self-seeking ways. The ultimate sacrifice made by Christ gives us another chance and acts as a buffer to the effects of our sinful ways. Through the fellowship of Twelve Step recovery and the community of believers, I have aligned myself with the Church. Now I also get to experience that connection in a lifelong relationship with my spouse. The *Catechism of the Catholic Church* outlines these opportunities without mincing words as it proclaims, "Marriage helps to overcome self-absorption, egoism, pursuit of one's own pleasure, and to open oneself to the other, to mutual aid and to self-giving." These are also the fruits of becoming entirely ready to have God remove our outlined defects of character through the sixth step of recovery. Both have helped transform a man who lacked any resemblance to marriage material into one who can wake up each morning and offer himself to serve the Lord, his wife, and his neighbor to the best of his ability, and in turn be offered the grace to get back up when he comes up short.

✝

Let Us Pray

God,
I stand before you with an open mind
and an open heart.
I come ready to believe
that you know what is best for me.
I am willing to shed all that you ask of me
so that my true self may be revealed
to you and to others.
I continue to believe that your will for me
is superior to the plans that I have for myself.
I am ready to become new
and clothed with the armor of your love.
Amen.

Going Further

1. What have you identified as the source of your hang-ups?
2. As you work through the steps, pause and reflect on some of the miracles that God has worked in your life. What do you see that you were unable to witness before?

3. How has your behavior changed in an effort to participate in the grace of these miracles?

4. Is there anything that you are still unwilling to let go of that you believe is integral to your ultimate happiness?

5. How willing and ready are you to have God remove all the defects of character that stand in the way of your usefulness to him and your fellows?

6. If your level of willingness is still low, spend time each day asking God for the willingness to be willing.

7.

A HUMBLE
REQUEST

Early in my recovery, I learned that the three qualities necessary for making this journey fruitful are humility, open-mindedness, and willingness (HOW). Humility is the one that I have struggled with most. Even the word itself was unfamiliar to me. In fact, when reminded that I needed to bring humility, open-mindedness, and willingness to a particular relationship that I was working to improve, I actually thought that the humility part meant that I was supposed to be humorous in some way, not even knowing that the word stemmed from *humble*. Ironically, for quite some time, I lacked the humility to admit that I wasn't sure what the word meant!

Since leaving home after high school, I had been working to forge my own destiny, and the results were what drove me to seek help. I was trying to play God in my life (and in the lives of others), and it didn't work out so well. Still, I thought that if only I tried harder or did a better job managing my life circumstances, I could get by. It took some time to realize that it required more than my own limited human faculties to achieve the spiritual awakening that I had been told was vital to finding long-term recovery. This was the same shift in approach, involving the same necessary qualities, that I had to bring into my relationship with God. Even as it related to my developing prayer life, I had to smash the idea that my prayers had to be worded in a particular way in order to be answered. The fears that I came to realize through working a thorough moral inventory in the fourth step continued to surface in ways that gave me opportunities to surrender them to God. By the time I broke ground on Step 7, humbly asking God to remove my shortcomings, I had pivotal moments in which to practice the art of surrender.[1]

One such experience that vividly comes to mind occurred in my first ninety days of sobriety. For most, this is a time marred by confusion, second-guessing, and daily battles against the urge to revert back to old habits in order to maneuver through emotional highs and lows. I was riding my bike around town when I saw my ex-girlfriend with her sister and brother-in-law, who were visiting from out of town. They were riding their bikes down the street about a half block away. Just the sight of them triggered in me a self-pity frenzy that I had a hard time shaking. It brought up feelings of loneliness, fear, and a compulsive urge to do something to arrange the situation. Becoming aware of all of this, while finding that these feelings were in direct contrast to the moments of serenity with which I was starting to become familiar, I reached for one of the new tools I was given. Rather than reacting immediately to this trigger, I pulled over and called my sponsor to talk with him about the situation and my rising anxiety. Just the act of picking up my phone and knowing that someone was there for me helped get me out of my loneliness. I asked for help and shared my plan with him, lacking any strategy but feeling the need to fix a situation that needed no immediate fixing.

"How do you feel right now, Scott?" he asked, puzzling me. Why did that even matter?

"I feel like I need to do something about this. I feel scared, lonely, and as if I will always be alone," I replied.

Trying to bring some levity to the situation, he half-jokingly suggested that I should be grateful that there wasn't a fourth biker, alluding to the fact that I didn't have to witness my ex-girlfriend with another man. "I suggest you go back home and sit on your hands for about fifteen minutes before doing anything." I hated that idea, but having agreed to go to any lengths to find recovery, I obliged. I biked back to my small studio apartment and took a seat on my bed, literally with my hands between the back fabric of my shorts and my unmade bed. I thought to myself initially, "Why am I doing this? I should be out there doing something about the situation. Anything!" Then I stewed in my self-pity for a little longer, contemplating all of the things that could have gone differently in my life if I had only been a bit more disciplined at a younger age. That thought transitioned into a grim outlook on the future. Doubting everything, I got stuck on how unhappy I would be for the rest of my life if this relationship didn't work out. Next, I was swept up by all of my insecurities regarding my professional life and the difficulties I would have providing for myself and my future family. The mental flogging was finally broken by the vibration coming from the phone in my front right pocket. It was my sponsor, following up with how I was doing.

After I tried to convey the horror of what was going through my mind, he slowly talked me off the ledge and asked me to return to the present moment. He reminded me that I was safe and that I had a lot to be grateful for. He also reiterated that God's hand can be found in the present, not by drifting off into the past or diving ahead into the future. It was necessary that I reach for the divine hand being extended to me in the moment and realize that I couldn't remove the pain of my experience on my own. That short phone call reminded me of the words I heard every morning at the start of the Twelve Step meeting I was attending: "For yesterday is but a dream, and tomorrow is only a vision, but each day well lived makes every yesterday a dream of happiness and every tomorrow a vision of hope. Look well, therefore, to this day."

Looking back on that moment, I can see how irrational thoughts were blown far out of proportion. There were several other times like this where a spiritual battle was taking place on the feelings plane. Each had its own variation and trigger, which, when left unchecked, hooked negative thoughts together that spiraled down into a dark pit. Whether the threat was real or unreal, it was the depression and reality that I got to know for extended moments of my life. For a long time, the only way I knew how to escape that dark chain of thoughts and feelings was to drink or do drugs. Suddenly, God began to take the place of those substances, and I was finding that all I had to do was sit on my hands and not get in the way. Humility was the key to this process, asking God to do for me what I could not do for myself. When I get caught too far in the past or the future, which I still do at times today, I am lacking the humility to allow God to be the driving force of my life. Even in my morbid reflection, it's a sign that I falsely believe I have a better understanding of how things should have gone or will go than my Creator does.

The gifts that God gives us, including the removal of our character defects, do not stop with us. They are an invitation to use what we have found in order to share hope with others. This is summarized beautifully in what is known as the Seventh Step Prayer:

> My Creator,
> I am now willing that you shall have all of me,
> good and bad.
> I pray that you now remove from me
> every single defect of character
> that stands in the way of my usefulness
> to you and my fellows.
> Grant me strength as I go out from here
> to do your bidding.
> Amen.

The Twelve Steps and personal recovery hinge upon the notion that we give back to God and others the great gifts that we have found in the process. This is also true of the Christian lifestyle, as rings throughout the command to love God and neighbor. Contrary to what I believed when I began my addiction recovery, the true source of humility does not lie in dramatic moments of humiliation. Instead, it is woven into the principle that God will direct our lives in order to bear fruit if we are open and willing to allow him to do so. The image of Christ as the vine and us as the branches, as depicted in the fifteenth chapter of the Gospel according to John, is the ultimate image of how humility works through the seventh step of recovery.

I am the true vine, and my Father is the vine grower. He takes away every branch in me that does not bear fruit, and every one that does he prunes so that it bears more fruit. You are already pruned because of the word that I spoke to you. Remain in me, as I remain in you. Just as a branch cannot bear fruit on its own unless it remains on the vine, so neither can you unless you remain in me. I am the vine, you are the branches. Whoever remains in me and I in him will bear much fruit, because without me you can do nothing. (Jn 15:1–5)

The truth behind the vine and branches clearly reveals our humble role as children of God. Within his grasp, we can do all that he inspires us to do. This is especially true for the recovering addict who has become sadly familiar with the rotting away that takes place when we are distant from Christ, the true source and salvation of our lives. As we grow through the course of our recovery, we are in regular need of divine pruning. This is made possible when we ready ourselves with just enough humility, open-mindedness, and willingness.

Engaging the Sacrament

As I traveled the road paved for me to fully enter the sacramental life of the Church, I came across a few roadblocks of my own making. Again, I approached my understanding of God's mercy with my own brokenness and human limitations, so finding justification for mercy was difficult. One particular hang-up I stumbled upon was the "car wash" understanding of confession I had. I have heard this as a critical assessment of how the Church offers forgiveness—how can God just clear away the sins of our past simply because we share them with another person? Doesn't that approach lack a necessary amount of justice? Perhaps, but that narrow conception also fails to encompass the entirety of the forgiveness process available through the Sacrament of Reconciliation. Viewing the sacrament in conjunction with the action taken in the seventh step of recovery, we can come to understand the fullness and beauty of distancing ourselves from our sinfulness and gazing toward forgiveness from God, others, and ourselves.

Somewhere in the process of the Twelve Steps of recovery and in the sacramental life of the Church lived properly, a radical change takes place. In recovery language, we call this a spiritual awakening or spiritual experience. In sacramental terms, we often refer to it as an interior conversion or conversion of the heart. In both cases, this tends to happen slowly over time—sometimes so subtly that others begin to take notice before we are capable of seeing it within ourselves. There are, of course, rare cases where this radical shift happens in a sudden "white light" type of experience. Let's not discount the miraculous ways God can offer change in our lives. When it comes to immersing ourselves in the fullness of the Sacrament of Reconciliation, we ought to be intentional about having a willingness to change our behavior and attitude. Stepping away from sin and rebuking evil within our hearts are the components that differentiate full cooperation with the grace offered by the Sacrament of Reconciliation from a quick wash-and-wax to get the filth off.

Christ calls out to this place of transition many times in the gospels. His first words in Matthew's gospel proclaim, "Repent, for the kingdom of heaven is at hand" (Mt 4:17). When asked why he ate and drank with tax collectors and sinners, he responded by saying, "Those who are healthy do not need a physician, but the sick do. I have not come to call the righteous to repentance but sinners" (Lk 5:31–32). In the parable of the lost son, we see a troubled young man who spent his inheritance and all that was given to him by his father. After hitting rock bottom, he experienced an interior repentance before returning to his father. "While he was still a long way off, his father caught sight of him, and was filled with compassion. He ran to his son, embraced him and kissed him" (Lk 15:20). God longs for our conversion to him. We get to encounter his merciful embrace within Reconciliation. Making a regular—even daily—return to the Lord with the humble awareness that we cannot find salvation on our own, open-mindedness to his will for us, and willingness to carry out that will keeps us properly aligned with the hope offered by God's grace and mercy.

We can take practical actions to remain in this state of continuous conversion. Outlined in the *Catechism of the Catholic Church* are several exercises that aid us on a regular basis. "Conversion is accomplished in daily life by gestures of reconciliation, concern for the poor, exercise and defense of justice and right, by the admission of faults to one's brethren, fraternal correction, revision of life, examination of conscience, spiritual direction, acceptance of suffering, endurance of persecution for the sake of righteousness. Taking up one's cross each day and following Jesus is the surest way of penance."[2]

This list offers a multitude of what my sponsor, Thomas, would call "estimable things." As I was going through the journey of picking up my cross daily and enduring the highs and lows of addiction recovery, I fell into a spiritual lull for a time. As I shared the morose state that I was in with the man I could trust with anything, we came to discover that my somber mood was going hand-in-hand with inaction. I was not doing the things that brought forth regular conversion in my daily life, and was feeling overwhelmed by my own sinfulness and a lack of self-esteem. "The best way to gain esteem is by doing estimable things," he began repeating to me on a regular basis. "You can't think your way into right action. You have to act your way into right thinking." Moments like these come and go, to varying degrees, for all who walk along spiritual paths. Several causes have been theorized, but even those deemed some of the holiest people that have walked the earth, such as St. Mother Teresa of Calcutta, have battled prolonged spiritual troughs. There is great virtue in taking action despite a lack of emotionally charged inspiration. I have also found comfort during these periods by coming to realize that I am not the only one who battles against natural undulations, and that I can unite myself with Christ and others in any suffering that takes hold when I am in the valley. As a recovering alcoholic and drug addict, I can also attain gratitude from the fact that I have better solutions to changes in my mood than my old ways of drinking heavily or doing drugs to avoid reality. I can count on the tools that have been freely given to me that help me show mercy to myself.

Some of the same tools have helped Janice along the road of recovery from unhealthy attachments to relationships, vanity, anxiety, bouts of self-hatred, and a tendency toward obsessive-compulsive disorder. Leaning on regular participation in the Sacrament of Reconciliation, she found that daily conversions help maintain the radical shift toward God her life has taken, which in turn provides her with the humility and willingness she needs to show empathy for others and give back where she can.

"I felt that I had a major conversion experience," she explained while commenting on the daily temptations that she fights against, "and I couldn't waste the suffering that I had been through as an invitation to God. I was feeling forgiveness from God for the terrible things that I had done, and he continues to forgive me. I can't do this alone, so getting closer to God plays a large part in where I am today. I want God to be proud of me. I want to live virtuously." Like the prodigal son who found himself in the loving embrace of his father, Janice yearns for the repeated encounters she has with God's mercy. Her life has become aligned in a way that is inspiring, and has begun to resemble the lives that many saints have led. Yet, she continues one day at a time to invite God into every area of her life, realizing that there is still room for improvement and further repentance. "Everything in my life has changed as a result of the relationship that I have with God: my job, my ability to have friends, what I do with my time, my career goals, my relationships. Everything is influenced by Christ, and the areas that have not been influenced are the areas in which I am still struggling, because I am failing to give those up to him for whatever reason." In Janice's life and in the lives of millions who have found recovery from addiction and other attachments, the kingdom of God is at hand.

✝

Let Us Pray

Lord,
I come before you to humbly ask
that you help remove my shortcomings.
Perhaps a beloved son (daughter) shall remain
to bear witness to the divine role
that you have had in my life.
Show me the grace to do this
through word and action.
I ask this not so I may be glorified
in the eyes of others,
but so that I may go forward
to do your will in all facets of my life.
Free me from impatience, stubbornness, and
pride, so that my life may fall in line with your
divine plan.
I truly believe that in your grasp, Oh Lord,
I can do all that you inspire me to do.
Amen.

Going Further

1. Are you equipped with the three necessary tools for personal change: humility, open-mindedness, and willingness? Explain.

2. Begin making an effort to live each day in the present, to the best of your ability. Develop habits of keeping your mind from wandering too far off into the past or too far ahead into the future. If you find yourself drifting, humbly return to God with a grateful and repentant heart.

3. When have you encountered a spiritual lull that has made getting into action difficult? How have you found success getting out of that lull in the past?

4. For the next several weeks, pray the Seventh Step Prayer on a daily basis:

> My Creator,
> I am now willing that you shall have all of me,
> good and bad.
> I pray that you now remove from me
> every single defect of character
> that stands in the way of my usefulness
> to you and my fellows.
> Grant me strength as I go out from here
> to do your bidding.
> Amen.

8.

WILLING TO
MAKE AMENDS

During the last several years, as I work through recovery, I have repeatedly heard this sound piece of advice: "The most important thing you will have to keep working on throughout your recovery will be your relationships." This has proven to be true, as relationships with others, with God, and with oneself are central to both the Twelve Steps of recovery and the grace offered by the sacraments. Step 8 suggests we make a list of all persons we have harmed, and become willing to make amends to each of them. This step offered me a practical approach to mending relationships that had been tarnished in the past and to laying a foundation for relationships I was beginning to build.

Having a new God consciousness forming within me, I started to realize that my actions were so often contrary to what God wanted for me. The actions of my past had separated me from those that cared about me deeply and unconditionally. Whether it was lying, stealing, or not showing up for holidays and other important events, my behavior had affected others, and there was more I had to do to reconcile the hurt I had caused. Prior to this slow transformation, I had justified my inappropriate behavior and reliance on drugs and alcohol by holding on to a perception of myself as victim of certain wrongs in my life. My resentments kept me from seeing my part in the pain and turmoil I was putting others and myself through. I was constantly pointing fingers.

There was a moment when I was twenty-one and in an inpatient treatment center in Wisconsin after my second DUI arrest. I checked myself in there mostly in an effort to appease my parents. During that stay, I was journaling about all the reasons I had to resort to drugs and alcohol instead of love and mercy. On a double-sided sheet of notebook paper, I outlined an idea for a book that I thought I would write. I still have that paper and now laugh about my intentions voiced in those scrawled notes. They were full of self-pity. Had I written that book, it should have been titled *If You Had My Problems, You Would Probably Be an Alcoholic Too.* It would have been a vastly different book from the one you are holding in your hand because I was still unwilling to let God into my life, to grow a relationship with him—not to mention the human relationships that I was destroying. As a result of my choice to stay distant from God, I returned to alcohol and drugs several months after leaving that treatment facility and returned to trying to manage my life on my own. Every excuse I could find to minimize the wrong I was doing I used as a tool to fuel the idea that I was a victim.

After working through Steps 4–7 with my sponsor, we put a plan in place to begin the amends process. It started with making a list of all the persons I had harmed. My sponsor suggested that I divide those people into three different groups: those that I was already willing to make amends to, those that I wasn't completely willing to make amends to, and the ones that I was in no way willing to get face-to-face with for whatever reason. While making this list, I became extremely alarmed by the idea that I would have to actually make a one-on-one admission to these people. At some prospects I shuddered, asking myself why I had to take ownership of my side of the street when they had contributed just as much, if not more, to the broken relationship. Feelings of embarrassment and fear of the truth were wrapped around my concerns about making amends to a few others, and I was in disbelief that I would be asked to reconnect with some people that had moved on far beyond the harm of our relationship. Instead of seeing the healing power that this process offered, I only saw my own image and reputation at risk. Resorting to honesty seemed unreasonable when the damage was done (long ago, in some cases) and the people in question were unlikely to want anything to do with me.

Over time, I have learned that these worries are entirely normal. Walking through this step with a sponsor is crucial to going through it gracefully and easing the pain associated with the prospect of coming clean about some of this stuff. We talked about how we would transition from Step 8 to Step 9, where the amends would actually take place (unless to do so would injure myself or others). But at the moment, my sponsor asked me to stay focused on the step in front of me, which included making the list of amends that needed to be made and then inviting prayer into the process.

Many wise thinkers and theologians have com-
mented that prayer does not change our situation;
rather, it changes us. I never exposed myself to that sort
of thinking before making a radical shift in my life, and
most of my experience with prayer prior to this time was
pleading with God to get me out of some mess I made
for myself. To overcome the seeming injustice of making
amends to those I still felt hurt by, it was strongly suggested that I pray for the people I was having difficulty
with. "Pray for them, even if you don't genuinely feel
what it is that you're praying for," was my sponsor's
advice. "Do this for three weeks, and let me know how
it goes." Contrary to how I felt about it, I prayed nightly
for those whom I still felt wronged by. I invited God to
grant them the peace and happiness that I seek in my
own life, and I united my prayer intentions with the
prayers and yearning of each of them. What invariably
happened as I combed through the individual prayers
I was bringing to God was that my heart started soft-
ening for those individuals. I began to look forward to
requesting their well-being and asked God to heal the
damage that I had caused in the relationship, knowing
that my part in the healing process would include cleaning up my side of the street. This approach radically
changed the way I mentally and emotionally reacted
to the thought of taking the next step, and helped me
maintain the necessary willingness to reconcile the relationships in my life.

The shame of my past still lingered, and I was regularly confronted with ideas of what my life "should"
have looked like. Even in the decisions that I made or the
actions that I failed to take in my recovery journey, I was
getting caught up in the things that should have been.

One day I was sharing these thoughts with my sponsor as he patiently listened to the laundry list of my regrets. Looking to him for confirmation of the shame that I was feeling in those moments, he simply glanced at me and said, "You're 'shoulding' yourself. When are you going to become willing to make amends to yourself and realize that there are things you *could* do while getting over the fact that you haven't done everything perfectly?"

Remembering that my relationship with myself also needed to be reconciled, I knew that coming to terms with my imperfections and flaws was going to be an important element of my addiction recovery. This didn't mean that I was going to condone and become complacent about my character defects, but that in order to be open to the love God has for me, I needed to be willing to accept that love despite the temptation to shame myself.

Making amends to myself started by getting in tune with the way that I was talking to myself. It was brought to my attention that if I spoke to others the way that I spoke to and of myself, I would be left with a lot more brokenness in my relationships. In order to heal the relationship I had with myself, I needed to do some things as simple as changing the words I used in my mind. Instead of reflecting on all the things I "should" have done, I came to see them as things I might have done. This attitude helped me stay in the moment without getting drawn too far into the past or coming to grips with what the future might hold. In an ironic way, it also helped me overcome bouts of procrastination, selfishness, and fear. This attitude opened up space where I could allow God to be a part of my status quo instead of wishing for what might have been. These lessons drew me closer to full reconciliation and aligned the work that I was doing on the eighth step of recovery with the opportunities that were continuing to open up through my experience with the other steps.

Engaging the Sacrament

Facing the damage that was caused by my self-centered behavior was instrumental in coming to understand the gravity of my sinful actions. As the shame I felt about the consequences of my decisions increased, it propelled me to learn that my actions had lasting effects on others. This insight moved me away from the propensity to sin again, which is a key aspect of the Sacrament of Reconciliation's penitential character. Sin is not just something that disrupts my relationship with God and damages my chances of one day being with him in heaven; it also harms my union with others and myself. In order to continue to find some interior justification for my addictive and sinful behaviors, I had spent a lot of time diminishing the impact of my actions. The idea of sin became less significant to me as I pushed it aside to find the source of what I thought would fulfill me. I was going to disturbing lengths to find a quick fix to my inadequacies, and often that meant feeling very little emotional impact for the way my actions affected others.

The self-seeking nature of sin, and the remorse God allows us to feel because of it, remind me of the gospel scene after Christ's arrest when Peter disowns Jesus. Peter had to repeatedly deny ever knowing Jesus before the weight of his sinfulness caught up to him. Even after Jesus foretold Peter's duplicity, Peter still denied knowing Jesus in the midst of Christ's suffering. Upon insisting that he did not know his Savior, Peter was brought to repentance by the grace-filled glance of the Lord: "He went out and began to weep bitterly" (Lk 22:62). I can't help but relate this incident to my years of denial regarding my alcoholism and drug addiction, as well as the reality that my sinfulness was damaging the lives of so many others. An addict that fights to manage and control his behavior for any length of time may also be able to relate. Peter found the temporarily painful dart that pierced his heart and brought him to an interior conversion. He was allowed to feel the emotional impact that his sinful conduct had on the Lord. He was given a chance for contrition.

Sin divides us from God and from others. It tears into the fabric of who we are and our ability to acknowledge ourselves as beloved sons and daughters of God. Some specific examples point to the pain that an addict's life can bring to others. The active alcoholic or drug addict may bring chaos to his home, largely shaping the lives of his spouse and children. A sex addict's impact on the lives of those he is close to may reveal itself in subtler ways at first, but the by-product of his addictive behavior has significant ramifications. Dr. Peter Kleponis, who works primarily with men in his counseling practice, speaks to this: "You look at the married man: the harm he's done to his marriage because he hasn't been able to be fully present to his wife. Or, maybe he's having sex but he is fantasizing about other women. Wives are definitely hurt by this. Children are hurt. So many times I've talked to men and they've said they have missed significant events in their kids' lives because they would rather be looking at porn instead of being at the school play or the baseball game. Careers have been hurt because instead of doing their jobs they are looking at pornography."

The interior conversion vital to the process of finding long-term recovery is guided by grace. We receive this grace through our efforts to distance ourselves from sin and create a life that is open to God's will. A contrite heart that shows sincere remorse directs us on the path that moves away from sin. This was something I learned when actively praying for those that I felt justified in harming when I was in the midst of working through the eighth step. Upon offering devoted time communicating with the Lord and praying for the intentions of those I had harmed, I was brought closer to a place where I was willing to do my part to bring justice to past situations by seeking forgiveness and showing genuine sorrow for the wrong that I had done.

The conclusion of our time in confession with a priest involves saying an act of contrition. A standard act of contrition reads something like, "My God, I am sorry for my sins with all my heart. In choosing to do wrong and failing to do good, I have sinned against you whom I should love above all things. I firmly intend, with your help, to do penance, to sin no more, and to avoid whatever leads me to sin." At first glance, this seems like a tall order that we are professing. What I have come to realize is that when we recite an act of contrition, we are making a commitment to participate in the grace that God is offering us through forgiveness and reconciliation with him. By becoming willing to make amends to all those that we have harmed, we are fulfilling the intention of doing penance that we proclaim through the Sacrament of Reconciliation. Participating in God's grace by performing the necessary penance, as well as doing our best to sin no more and avoid the near occasion of sin, can only occur through divine aid. My previous perception of Reconciliation as a Catholic car wash approach to cleaning ourselves of sins was gone by the time I started preparing to make amends. If this was a car wash, I was being asked to get inside myself and shampoo the carpets, restore the vinyl, and make a commitment to do my best not to bring any dirt back inside. I must say, though, that the process of finding healing through the forgiving love of Reconciliation is a lot like getting into and driving a brand-new car!

Equally as powerful in the process of getting face-to-face with a priest, who acts in *persona Christi* (the person of Christ), is the dialogue we can engage in after the confession of sins. This is a chance to receive direction about the path to take in order to break free from our sinful nature and to make progress in recovery from our brokenness. While coming to understand our situation, the priest suggests an appropriate penance to satisfy our sinfulness. He then grants us absolution for our sins and will also guide us through the steps needed to heal the effects of our sins. Just as we prepare to make amends in Step 8 of the Twelve Steps, our sacramental penance brings justice and recovery from the damage that our sinful behavior creates. Simply confessing our sins to God, which helps us acknowledge our need for forgiveness, lacks this component that helps us journey to full restoration of the relationships that are vital to our existence.

†

Let Us Pray

Our Creator,
I am humbled by the great gifts
that you have placed in my life,
particularly the willingness to grow
in my relationships.
Thank you for your pursuit of me
I am grateful for the chance to amend
relationships
that have gone sour.
I ask for the necessary humility
to see my part in these relationships, and ask for
the willingness
to make things right with those I have harmed.
I pray that the intentions of others be fulfilled
so that they may find the same degree
of happiness and satisfaction from this life
that I seek for myself.
Amen.

Going Further

1. Where do you stand in your relationship with God,
    your relationship with others, and your relationship
    with yourself?
2. How have these relationships improved over the
    past several months?
3. What are some of the effects that your behavior has
    had on aspects of your life for which you may not
    yet have accounted?
4. Make a list of all persons you have harmed. Divide
    this list into three columns: those that you are will-
    ing to make amends to, those that you are possibly

willing to make amends to, and those that you will certainly not make amends to.

5. Begin praying for each individual on your list, especially those that you still hold resentments toward. Ask God for the willingness to see your part in the tarnished relationship.

9.

DIRECT AMENDS
TO THOSE WE
HAVE HARMED

There was a moment when I first started meeting regularly with my sponsor when he asked me a very simple yes or no question. He would remind me of my answer to the question whenever I lost the ambition to work the next step. He inquired, "Are you willing to go to any lengths to achieve sobriety?" Driven by the pain that I was going through that brought me to my knees and had me seeking fellowship with others who had found a solution to our common problem, I responded with an emphatic, "*Yes!*" When I got to Step 9, which suggests we make direct amends to the people we have harmed (outlined in Step 8) wherever possible, except when to do so would injure them or others, I was reminded of my initial commitment to go to any lengths to achieve sobriety. Up to this point, I heard stories of relapses that had taken place amongst those willing to share their experience with me. It seems as though the people that do not find the courage to complete the ninth step are often the people that resort back to their old ways, and usually they find themselves drunk, high, and worse off than when they started. With my list in front of me, I began working through how I would make amends to those that I felt would be easier to approach. Again, I didn't haphazardly do this on my own. I was given encouragement and guidance from my sponsor.

The amends that I made came in various forms. In some cases, it was appropriate to write a letter to the person I had harmed, giving details that would be helpful in the healing process and taking ownership for my part in the tarnished relationship. In other situations, I made amends in person. For these, it was recommended that I request a time and place where we could comfortably talk with each other in an intimate way and that I provide some notice about the nature of my visit. There are some amends that I have not completed, either because the prudent time has not been made available or because it was deemed through the spiritual counsel of my sponsor that doing so would bruise the other even more. In these cases, I have been actively working to maintain a "living amends," a commitment to shape my lifestyle so that I will no longer hurt that person or others in a similar way. While not perfect, I gain esteem by knowing that I have shown progress in my life by living with an adjusted outlook that is driven by God consciousness.

I found that it was crucial that I not get defensive during the process of making amends. I was to point out the wrong that I had done, ask for forgiveness, and consult to find out if there was anything more I could do to make things right. Making excuses, justifying my behavior, and defending myself were not in the formula. At times it was hard to bite my tongue. My ego wanted to remind others that I perceived my actions as merely a reaction to the wrong that I had experienced. To combat this temptation, my sponsor asked me to draft a letter to each person I was making amends to, even those I would see face-to-face. When I completed each letter, he read it and crossed off some portions. Either because I was only giving half the truth or because I was trying to shift blame to other people or situations, he asked me to rewrite the parts that were crossed off. In some cases, I had to compose three or four drafts! This exercise taught me the value of taking full ownership of the wrong that I had done and enabled me to make a complete and genuine effort to repair the damage I had done in the lives of those I cared about, at least to the best of my ability.

Thomas, who is more than twenty years removed from his last drink and drug (which was an attempt at overdose in his apartment by himself), shares his struggles in working the ninth step.

> As I continue to work through the steps over and over, my struggle continues to be controlling people, places, and things. Playing the director. If everyone is in the right place, if everyone is doing the right things, then I am going to be happy. Although I stopped drinking and drugging, that behavior was still very much a part of me and my ego. I was still fearful. I still had some belief that if I could just get all of these things, have people act in a certain way, and keep things in the right order, then I would be happy. Of course, I was dead wrong and left frustrated, irritable, and discontented just as if I was drinking. It became obvious that I needed to accept my powerlessness over people, places, and things while focusing on the things that I can change, which is my attitude. I regularly need to do *my* housecleaning and work on myself. That

means taking responsibility for the mess I have
made and make direct amends wherever possible.
I have tried to control outcomes as well as people,
places, and things. In the end, it's just an illusion.
Control is nothing but fear-based illusion. You can
call it delusion.

Making amends for the wrongs they have done
is a consistent effort for those who have lived through
decades of quality recovery. Thomas's commitment to
go beyond freedom from drugs and alcohol to a continuous self-examination has encouraged me to constantly
reflect on my habits and see where my side of the street
needs to be cleaned up. Pointing fingers at others is the
easy way, but I committed to go to any length to achieve
sobriety. That also means going to any length to distance
myself from sin and the root of what divides me from
others.

Engaging the Sacrament

Making reparation for the wrong that we have committed acts as a springboard into a new way of life that is
full of meaning. It creates an eye for others that looks
past selfish ambition and seeks to unify. Prior to getting
sober, I was one of very little faith. After a few months
of placing my life in the hands of God, I was discovering what faith truly was. Upon working the ninth step
of recovery and committing myself to the penance that
filled my contrite heart, I was now merging faith and
works: "Just as a body without a spirit is dead, so also
faith without works is dead" (Jas 2:26). There were several times when I was unwilling to take the prescribed
dose of penance for my wrongs, and I believe that God

acted graciously to answer my prayers for increased willingness.

As we slowly shed the layers of self-centeredness (that still return every day), they are replaced by what the Church considers the four cardinal virtues: *prudence, justice, fortitude,* and *temperance.* All four have been essential to the process of making amends to those I have harmed, and each enables us to make appropriate reconciliation with God, others, and ourselves. We can receive a share in these virtues through the sacramental life of the Church.

Prudence, which guides judgment based on sound reasoning, is a necessary aspect of discerning what amends are to be made and how we go about making them. In my experience, I gain prudence by leaning on a core group of individuals that can help objectively weigh any decision I am making. Fellowship that is rooted in Christ can help cultivate the virtue of prudence, and as we acknowledge the will of God in our lives, we become more in tune with the Spirit, who guides our judgment.

Justice is the result of doing what is right in the face of our fallen nature. Making amends to the ones we have harmed, not so that we may hold our head high and feel good about ourselves, but because we desire the well-being of the other, requires justice. Praying that our neighbor receives all the peace and serenity that we desire for ourselves is a gateway to justice, just as preparing for our amends with a contrite heart unites us with the impact of our sinfulness. The search for justice begins with assessing our conduct on a regular basis and taking measures to keep ourselves from the near occurrence of sin, especially when it becomes habitual. There are a few people on my amends list that I will never get the chance to make things right with because doing so would cause more damage in their lives or in the lives of others. In these cases, I have had to make a commitment to God and myself to resist the temptation that drove me to hurt that person, so that I will not repeat this behavior with someone else. In situations where I have betrayed my relationship with God and others to seek my own temporary pleasure, I have made a habit of regularly asking God to relieve me of the bondage of selfishness that harms others. For example, there are a few women on the list of people that I have harmed by my sexual desires who would only be hurt further if I wiggled my way back into their lives for a moment just to help me recover. Some have husbands and families, and breaking into their lives so that I can check their name off my list would be selfish and unjust. Prudence has helped form layers of justice in my life.

Fortitude is a cardinal virtue that offers the strength to persist through moments of great fear and difficulty. It unveils itself when we are tempted to take the easier, softer way in overcoming the root of our addictions and unhealthy attachments. Fortitude strengthens our commitment to go to any lengths to find sobriety, and to ensure that our recovery is the foundation upon which everything else in our lives rests. Getting through the first ninety days of sobriety from any addiction, while attending the suggested ninety meetings in ninety days, requires a fortitude that most recovering addicts are not familiar with until faced with the horrors of rock bottom. For many, fortitude stems from practicing a new set of routines to combat the life of hell they have recently escaped.

Temperance is the fruit of recovery. Depending on the addiction or unhealthy attachment that you seek healing from, you may call it sobriety. In other cases— although, in my own life, this would not hold true with regard to drugs and alcohol—temperance may be seen as moderation. Temperance can be developed through seemingly small acts, such as refraining from a second cookie, avoiding a second, lust-driven glance at someone of the opposite sex, or not hitting the snooze alarm in the morning. I have found that when I practice temperance in other areas of my life, the urges that fuel my addiction fade. Still, I have a lot of personal room for growth in the virtue of temperance.

Each of these virtues contributes to the upright way of living that is strengthened and nurtured through the grace of Reconciliation. Penance, amends, and bringing justice to situations that have been filled with havoc shape the way we live and move forward with our lives. They help build the freedom that, much like a life of virtue, we may have never considered possible for ourselves. These virtues are only made possible through God, and can be sustained by receiving our daily bread.

✝

Let Us Pray

Lord,
Because of the Sacrament of Reconciliation
and following the guidance of my heart,
I feel moved to bring justice
to the situations I once harmed.
Please continue to forgive me for the chaos
I have caused

Unite me with the suffering of your Son, Jesus
Christ,
as I right my wrongs through your grace.
Grant me prudence, justice, fortitude,
and temperance as I go forth to do your will.
Amen.

Going Further

1. How has your relationship with those on your amends list changed, if only within yourself, since making your list?

2. Find a sponsor or spiritual guide familiar with the principles of the Twelve Steps to help you through making your amends. Use prudence to determine which situations would be made worse and cause harm to those you have hurt or others if you were to make amends.

3. Who are the people that you are most willing to make amends to?

4. Begin setting a date and time to make direct amends to these people.

5. Who are those that you may have difficulty making amends to?

6. With the direction of your sponsor, start preparing yourself to make amends to those people when possible, praying for the willingness to do so when necessary.

EUCHARIST

10.

CONTINUED PERSONAL INVENTORY

The first Twelve Step meeting I attended in October 2011 is a bit of a blur to me. I do recall the madness (laughter and joy) that I heard from above as I reached the stairs leading up to the meeting room, followed by the mystery of others nonchalantly identifying themselves with the condition that was killing me. However, I do not remember anything about the content of what was shared in that hour-long gathering. What will be forever ingrained in my memory is what happened to conclude the meeting. We all gathered in a circle, held hands or put arms around each other's shoulders, and recited one of the few prayers I knew from my childhood. Together we proclaimed:

> Our Father who art in heaven,
> hallowed be thy name.
> Thy kingdom come.
> Thy will be done on earth, as it is in heaven.
> Give us this day our daily bread,
> and forgive us our trespasses,
> as we forgive those who trespass against us,

and lead us not into temptation,
but deliver us from evil.
For thine is the kingdom, the power,
and the glory forever.
Amen.

When we got to "hallowed be thy name," my walls
came down and I began to shed a tear. The familiarity
of it, the Spirit that was present in that moment, and a
sense of unity overwhelmed me to the point where I
felt that I really belonged. I felt that I was at home, and
I could trust the process of what was going to take place
next. Little did I know that the words we were praying
together detailed the way of life that the millions who
had found recovery before me live by.

Step 10 suggests that we continue to take personal
inventory and, when we are wrong, promptly admit it.
Steps 10, 11, and 12 are considered by some as mainte-
nance steps, to be practiced regularly. Every day. They
provide the guidelines for our new way of life that is
participation in the grace God has granted us through
the first nine steps. This is crucial because building
strength and aiming at a sustained spiritual awakening
are not one-time events. Just as I can't spend four hours
working out every January and expect that the physical
strength I build during that time will provide physical
fitness for the entirety of the year, the Twelve Steps need
ongoing commitment.

Recovery focuses our efforts on what we can do
today to participate in the grace that God provides us.
In the first few days and weeks, this truth reveals itself
in staving off the nearly impossible urge to drink, use
drugs, reach for pornography, go on an eating binge,
make one more wager, or indulge in whatever other

addiction or attachment that is your drug of choice. As the obsession to reach for that drug of choice fades and we begin clothing ourselves with the armor of God, the day-at-a-time approach to recovery means practicing on a daily basis the principles given to us through the Twelve Steps. This begins with a daily inventory inspired by a newly found God consciousness.

What is God consciousness? Let's define it as self-awareness wrapped up in a heart that continues to desire interior conversion. To maintain the fire that the Spirit places within our hearts, a personal inventory helps us determine when we are staying on the path laid out for us and when we start giving in to the temptation to resort to old behaviors. There are a few different ways to go about this inventory. Some people use a detailed rubric that helps them examine their actions and intentions at the conclusion of each day. Other reflections may be rooted in what Christ calls the two greatest commandments of all. From this perspective, you may retire at night asking yourself, "At what moments of my day did my actions and intentions reflect my love for the Lord with all my heart, mind, and soul? When did they fail to do so? Furthermore, how did my behavior show love for my neighbor as I wish to be loved? When did I come up short?" Notice that as we take our daily inventory, we do not simply keep a list of the things we have done wrong. It is also important to affirm the positive choices we have made and the intentions behind them. Each day will provide a series of successes and opportunities for growth that we can measure and strive for. Making this daily assessment a routine shapes the way we view our lives with the aid of God's vision.

Personal awareness of our conduct does not need to wait until the end of each day. In many cases, I have found it beneficial to make a quick assessment of what I am going through when things get heated in argument, when I isolate, when I doubt myself, or when I get caught up in envy. Moments like these give me the opportunity to identify my motivations and see what inspirations are of God and what are not of God. For some reason, I have a propensity to want to get the upper hand in situations. When I am taking a regular inventory of myself, I can recognize these moments as a spiritual attack from the forces of evil that seek to divide and separate me from God and others. Prayerful self-discovery aids in putting some space between the triggers, or stimuli that can set us off, and our reactions to them so that we may invite the will of God into our response.

In my relationships, I sometimes recognize thoughts that result in my pitting myself against someone. I seem to lie in wait, ready to use the thought as ammunition to get some kind of upper hand. Sometimes I catch this compulsion right away and let the thought pass by, dismissing it as ungodly. But at other times, the pain of this mental ping-pong has to get really bad before I come to realize that I have some interior work to do. Instrumental in moments like these is the willingness to keep my own side of the street clean. The hurt that we experience, even when provoked by the actions of others, indicates that something is unbalanced within ourselves. Sharing these feelings with a sponsor or trusted companion, especially when these moments of hurt occur regularly, helps us find solutions to the root of the problem and further unites us with God.

A tenth-step inventory also helps us form a structure of accountability that may be new to many who are coming out of the depths of self-seeking suffering. It was very new to me when I began the journey, and has been something I have had to hold tightly to in order to avoid slipping into keeping secrets, isolating, and resorting back to drugs and alcohol. Janice shares a similar point about the constant self-discovery she finds through the gifts and fellowship surrounding her: "Forming close relationships with other women gave me a much-needed second opinion. The big thing was the community—the relationship of people where I was actually held accountable, yet affirmed in what I was doing and the progress I was making—what I was doing well and what I could do well. My church community affirmed my gifts and abilities. I have been called to share my gifts with people, and could never have done that by myself. When I was isolated, that stuff never came up because I could not see it myself."

It is important to underscore the unifying aspect of the Twelve Steps. It's hard to be unified when we are not willing to be honest and to chisel that honesty to form our true selves in the eyes of God. In addition to the value of learning to be okay with the honest truth, I have seen it create a beautiful sense of confidence in those that are willing to accept themselves and situations around them exactly as they are. Acceptance doesn't necessarily mean approval or becoming idle. When joined with honesty, it means being able to share with God, ourselves, and others exactly who we are and what we are going through. "This is me, exactly who I am at this moment," is a proclamation that keeps shame from dwelling within us and puts trust in the will of God. Understanding the importance of a regularly taken inventory, Janice notes, "If I'm not honest with God, myself, or other people, I become very isolated and will become depressed or anxious. Spiritually, I become bored and frustrated. One flaw that I struggle with through my condition and tendency to seek approval of others is a lot of anger. Anger toward my condition, toward myself for what I did, and toward other people who I see have things I don't. I can also get angry at God. Not being honest about that anger creates isolation. I turn inward and then sin."

As my personal prayer life has developed, I have learned to use this honesty in my dialogue with God. It frees me to share with him where I am in certain situations, and takes away some of the power that those feelings had over me. I can prayerfully share with God the fact that I am feeling angry, envious, or mistreated. This honesty helps me engage the tools I have learned through seeking God's will and not trying to call all of the shots, even in my prayer requests. Simply bringing the fact that I am scared to prayer helps calm me and allows me to be okay with that. My propensity to judge my insides by other people's outsides lessens. "Thine is the kingdom, the power, and the glory forever."

Engaging the Sacrament

God deeply desires our union with him. The sacraments are gifts, handed down through the ministry of Jesus Christ, that bring about a tangible union with him here on earth. There is no more significant opportunity to join that union than in the Sacrament of the Eucharist. It heals, forms community, forgives, humbles, gives hope, and helps us reclaim our right order and right size. Countless experiences with the Eucharist have alleviated the destruction in my life caused by sin, specifically as it relates to pride, envy, shame, and frustration.

One story that has been especially influential in my own life and the lives of thousands of others is that of Maura Preszler. Throughout her childhood and into college, Maura had a number of demons to face. She suffered both physical and sexual abuse, struggled with an eating disorder that could have taken her life, battled her identity as a woman, and was diagnosed with depression, borderline personality disorder, and chronic post-traumatic stress disorder. Despite all of those things, Maura received healing in her early twenties.

"I was anorexic in high school and bulimic in college. Every morning in college, I just woke up and told myself I'm never going to do this again. This is the last day, and I'm going to get help. It didn't happen," Maura said, as she reflected back on her seemingly hopeless condition. She made many attempts to control things on her own. She planned her meals, eating them as she prescribed herself during the day, then often lost it at the end of the night. She tried eating with other people during the day, either with other athletes or students, but failed to keep it together. One day after attending daily Mass, she was on the floor of the chapel thinking to herself, "I need help. I cannot do this."

"I've been Catholic my whole life, but definitely did not live a very Catholic lifestyle. I didn't always believe what the Eucharist was, but there was just something about the Eucharist every day that gave me peace. I didn't know why I always ended up there, but I did—especially in eucharistic adoration. I always found myself at the chapel where I went to school. No matter what had happened on any given day, I felt some sort of peace there so I kept going back."

As many of us do, whether addicts or not, Maura found herself in the trap of comparing what was going on inside of her with others who she perceived had it all together. She then found someone who shared many of the same struggles, much as I found Michael and Brock early in my recovery process. "There was this one girl in particular who would always meet me there," Maura described. "She was really struggling with depression. It helped me when I opened up, and I started to see people for who they really were." Maura began to feel less alone, especially when she was able to relate small victories in her day. "She was so compassionate. It was really comforting to have someone else understand my pain. She suffered greatly from depression and so did I. When I told her, 'I brushed my teeth today, and that was a big deal,' she knew what I meant. It was very comforting and reassuring."

A lot of good can come from finding professional help with counselors and psychiatrists. Maura entrusted herself to a psychological institute on the East Coast where she was able to get a full diagnosis of her mental and emotional conditions as they related to her eating disorder, depression, borderline personality symptoms, and post-traumatic stress. She began to realize why she continued to get into romantic relationships, then push people away with the things she said or did. With the evidence laid out in front of her, she surrendered to the fact that she wasn't able to fight things on her own any longer. She learned she couldn't control much, but that she could control her ability to see the beauty within, and it began to change her perspective.

"I believe that everyone struggles and that everyone suffers to varying degrees. It's what we decide to do with that struggle that can either lift us up or bring us down. You're not going to meet someone who doesn't have a struggle. It may be a struggle with eating, alcoholism, pride, anger, or greed. With God's grace, we can cooperate with him and turn that weakness into what I believe can be our greatest strength. When I discovered that, it really changed my perspective and how I viewed my cross. Every day I get up, put my cross on my shoulder, and carry it to heaven." Maura paused for a moment with her young son on her lap as she shared this perspective with me. "Literally, Jesus tells us to get up and carry our cross. We can go through life and be bitter, angry, and resentful. However, that anger and resentment is only going to hurt us. It's not going to provide any quality of life, joy, or peace."

Introspection can be very challenging, yet incredibly rewarding and necessary to form a foundation for recovery. The inner work needed to find healing involves an honest look at ourselves on a daily basis, forgiveness, and erasing blame. For Maura, this meant letting go of the perfect childhood that she envisioned for herself but never had. She had to dig through a lot of pain in order to get to the other side. As a runner and collegiate athlete, she compares her healing to the preparation needed to compete. "It's like running a marathon. You don't just show up one day and run a marathon. It's the training, the early mornings, and the runs before the race that really count." Regular spiritual practices helped bring her toward healing and freedom from anxiety, depression, and nightmares. "I had to get over blaming myself for so many things that had happened that were out of my control. It was really freeing to do that, and I found a lot of healing when I learned to forgive myself. Having mercy on myself and knowing that I don't have to be perfect allows me to strive for grace. Every day is like a lifetime in recovery."

Forming a humble vision of God was also a key component to the new life that Maura found. Growing up, she admits to struggling with a very skewed view of her Higher Power. "My recovery led me to such a beautiful relationship with God the Father and helped me feel grateful for the cross, because I need it to know God in the way that I know him. I went to the Eucharist to find Christ. I was super bold, and would go in to adoration and speak to him very frankly. In the silence he answered. It led me to a deeper understanding of who he is and how much he loves me."

Rest assured that a relationship with God through the power of the Eucharist does not happen overnight. It's a mystery that we tend to complicate with our limited human understanding and very human efforts to attempt to know everything and have all the answers. This gradual development of a relationship with the Eucharist happened over the course of a year that Maura spent in Calcutta, India, while in college. It was the first time she ever prayed a Holy Hour in front of the Eucharist, and she had a hard time sitting still. Someone there spoke to her about God the Father, and the love that radiated from the guidance she received helped Maura overcome her lack of understanding. "I couldn't comprehend what this missionary was saying about God. She told me that if I want to get to know God, I should spend time with him as I would spend with a friend. From that time, I went and sat in adoration for an hour and kept doing it. A week turned into a month, a month turned into a year, and I kept going. My time in front of the Eucharist during adoration was just as important as therapy. In our culture, we need to be still. Reflective silence has been critical in my recovery."

A discussion of the tenth step, and the significance of the Eucharist in continuing to take personal inventory, must include a few words on gratitude. The *Catechism of the Catholic Church* expresses this well: "The Eucharist is a sacrifice of thanksgiving to the Father, a blessing by which the Church expresses her gratitude to God for all his benefits, for all that he has accomplished through creation, redemption, and sanctification. Eucharist means first of all 'thanksgiving.'"[1] The Eucharist provides our daily nourishment, similar to the fruits of a daily inventory, as the *Catechism* goes on to say: "Daily conversion and penance find their source and nourishment in the Eucharist, for in it is made present the sacrifice of Christ which has reconciled us with God. Through the Eucharist those who live from the life of Christ are fed and strengthened."[2]

I have heard it said many times that a grateful addict does not return to her drug of choice. This gratitude stems from the experience of hell that we go through in the throes of our addiction. "I've experienced hell, and I have no intention of ever going back there," is a saying I have heard more than once from individuals who have found freedom from addiction. A reminder of where we have been and the new chance at life that God has given us can typically instill in us the willingness needed each day to embrace our cross and carry it with gratitude. I have had several moments in recovery when my focus has diverted from the beautiful life that God has made for me to the one or two things that I am still unhappy about. Our Creator is painting a magnificent portrait of my life and has given me all the tools that I need to embrace his love and serve others. It is a far cry from what my life was like before, yet at times I find my focus drifting toward the unfinished edge. When my attention is given to that part of my life, I get bound up in frustration and have a tendency to forget all that I should be grateful for.

One day in particular comes to mind when I look back on the road of recovery. A few years ago, I was in a place where I was starting to pick up the pieces from the damage left by my active alcoholism and drug abuse. I had gotten back into school at a local community college to mend my grade point average, which had tanked immediately when I entered college and put my efforts into fulfilling the needs of my addiction rather than completing my schoolwork and working toward academic success. Several further attempts at college while I was trying to manage my drinking and drug use left me with the same results: incomplete classes, failed grades, withdrawals, and a college résumé that made it very difficult to get back into a four-year university. I was in the midst of my fifth semester of community college, which found me on the dean's list each term since I was free of my addictive behavior. After completing two or three semesters with grades that I could be proud of, I began applying to four-year universities to complete my bachelor's degree. Each application I sent in to local colleges was returned with a rejection letter, expressing regret that the school could not admit me and suggesting that I take measures to improve my grades and try again later. Each time I received one of these letters, I experienced disappointment, varying degrees of self-pity, but usually an improved motivation to continue the work that I was doing. In April 2014, I received yet another one of these letters and was fed up. "There aren't really any more classes I can take to improve my grade point average. What else can I possibly do?" It was a moment when I questioned the path that God was paving for me.

My depressed thinking added these college rejections to all the other negative ideas it could find, so that my thoughts spiraled into a frenzy of doubt and anxiety. A relationship that I had just gotten out of was left unsettled, leaving doubt and feelings of loneliness. A recent job opportunity that I was hoping for was given to someone else, which magnified my insecurities about the status of my schooling and stirred up old regrets. With all of this bouncing around my head, I went to a Twelve Step meeting to quiet my mind. It helped, but the chatter came back shortly after I left the meeting that evening. I then drove past my church parish and recalled that eucharistic adoration was being offered. I stepped in to pray in front of the Blessed Sacrament, doing the best I could to put my anger, self-pity, and disgruntled emotions into the hands of God. I made a commitment to stay open to what was in store for me, although I had my doubts that things would work out.

Somewhere in the midst of all my self-seeking thoughts and feelings, I was reminded of the date. It was April 10, 2014. Exactly two years earlier, I was celebrating six months of sobriety from drugs and alcohol. My mother had given me a token (an outward sign of an inward conversion that is exchanged in some recovery groups) as I celebrated with others who have found freedom from a similar condition. My mom cried plenty of tears of joy that day, as did I with the prospect of a new life beginning to unfold. At the thought of this, a smile came to my face and my heart began to warm. Kneeling in front of the Body of Christ, I was reminded that the day marked two and a half years of continuous sobriety from alcohol and drugs. It wasn't so much the milestone that mattered, but the rekindled joy and gratitude that God granted me that evening. As I look back on all of those things that I did not get at the time—the job, the relationship, acceptance into college—I see that God had other plans. If one or more of those things would have gone the way that I was sure it needed to go, there is a good chance that I would not have had the opportunity to found a Catholic nonprofit organization that seeks to help individuals and communities overcome the difficulty of addiction. It is also likely that an opportunity to share my story and the stories of others in book form would not have been presented to me. It is easier to suggest than to follow, but I urge you to be patient with the plans that God has for you. You never know what he has in store as the next door opens.

Everything that is good in my life is contingent upon my willingness to stay open to the will of God—which first and foremost means staying sober. As Dorothy and others expressed to me early on, my recovery must never be something that is on my plate, but rather must be the plate upon which everything else in my life rests. That requires union with God, who gives me the grace to remain sober one day at a time, and finding communion with him and others through the sacraments of the Church. I must never forget who I am—an alcoholic and drug addict that has found recovery through the miraculous work of my Higher Power. I am also a beloved son of God, with whom he is well pleased. Living in that space is a recipe for the gratitude that is a hallmark of those who have lived to share about long-term sobriety.

One last helpful piece of advice about cultivating gratitude—apart from reception of the Eucharist and the daily inventory suggested by Step 10—is to make a gratitude list. There are a few different ways to go about reminding oneself of things to be grateful for in one's life, and I have often used this trick on the fly when hit by some kind of disturbance that has me feeling pained or unjustly treated. In addition to repeating the Serenity Prayer time over time, I also got into the habit early on of reciting a gratitude list during difficult moments. One way I do this is by going through the alphabet, citing something that starts with each letter that I can be grateful for. For instance, today I am grateful for *a*lcoholism, which fuels my faith life and need to surrender. I am grateful for *b*ooks that have given me insight into the nature of recovery and the wisdom to know God in a deeper way. Thank God for my friend Chris, who has been a loyal companion throughout my faith journey and who provides both encouragement and laughter on a regular basis. I am grateful for my *d*ad, who has taught me so much throughout my life, including how to swing a golf club and throw a baseball. He has been supportive of me from a young age and gave me life. The list goes on and on . . .

Usually by the time I hit G or H, I have forgotten about what was bothering me and feel assured that God will continue to guide me through whatever may come my way. Others jot down three or four things that they are grateful for before heading to bed at night or begin their day with a gratitude list, mustering the necessary humility to live each day successfully in the eyes of God. Regardless of how we cultivate it, gratitude brings us closer to God. It is with gratitude that I recite, "Lord, I am not worthy that you should enter under my roof, but only say the word and my soul shall be healed," before uniting myself with Christ in the Eucharist.

✝

Let Us Pray

> Our Father who art in heaven,
> hallowed be thy name.
> Thy kingdom come.
> Thy will be done on earth, as it is in heaven.
> Give us this day our daily bread,
> and forgive us our trespasses,
> as we forgive those who trespass against us,
> and lead us not into temptation,
> but deliver us from evil.
> For thine is the kingdom, the power,
> and the glory forever.
> Amen.

Going Further

1. What are the daily commitments you have made to participate in the grace that God gives you today?
2. What reminders of God's grace have come into your life recently? How have you found your way back to him as a result?
3. In what circumstances have the issues of pride, envy, shame, and frustration made their way into your life?

4. Using your own personal rubric or one that is described in this chapter, begin taking a daily inventory. If moments appear where you have wronged someone, humbly admit it as soon as possible.

5. What things are you doing right on a regular basis?

6. Begin a routine of making a gratitude list, creating an accessible way to recall the great gifts God has placed in your life.

11.

CONSCIOUS CONTACT
WITH GOD

Prayer can be a very intimate act when given one's full attention. When I bring the three key elements of recovery into my prayer life—humility, open-mindedness, and willingness—I am often blown away by what comes from my honesty with God and the strength that is provided when I truly seek his will for me. I used to complicate prayer and set an expectation that I needed to be in a certain realm of holiness in order to enter deeply into prayer. Not only that, but I associated the idea of meditation with my kale-eating, yoga-practicing, legs-shaped-in-a-pretzel friends that saw themselves as spiritual rather than religious. By giving it a chance and following the prescribed basic outline of Step 11, namely, that "we sought through prayer and meditation to improve our conscious contact with God as we understood him, praying only for the knowledge of his will for us and for the power to carry that out," I was able to get some traction on the phrase, "Thy will be done."

Many of us have past experience with prayer, often early in our lives. Perhaps we only resort to prayer as a last attempt at getting out of a certain situation or avoiding the consequences of our misbehavior. If your experience is like mine, you have tried negotiating with God through prayer, making promises in return for some short-term outcome. "God, if you do exist, please get me out of this situation. Just this one time! I promise I will never do that again if you help me out of this jam." Sound familiar? Sometimes these requests are answered the way we want; other times, they are not. Either way, in my past I had always forgotten about my end of the bargain and was happy to have God, if he existed, squeeze me out of another dilemma. Then, naturally, I would revert back to the same type of behavior that got me into the jam. It was insanity.

The most important aspect of prayer and meditation, through the work of Step 11, is trying not to bend God's will toward mine. Rather, prayer is a practice of becoming willing to bend my will toward that of the Lord. I can get caught up in all of my personal requests—which in themselves are okay as long as they serve God and work toward building the kingdom of heaven. But when I am praying to God with a wish list like he's Santa Claus, then I know that I am trying to take my will back and call the shots as if I know what is better for me than God does. In these scenarios, I typically find myself praying for comfort, which ironically is the same thing I sought when I was deep in the melee of my alcoholism and drug addiction. It is in moments of distress that I see my need to rely on God and open myself to his will. I have seen this lesson unfold in my other relationships as well. When my friends and I began inviting each other into our prayer lives, it was a tangible way of asking God to be a part of our relationships. Don't get me wrong; group prayer was a bit awkward at first, but it became a safe place where we could share our innermost grumblings—that perhaps only God could understand—with each other. We didn't claim to have the answers, but put faith in God's vision for how healing in our world could take place.

My relationship with Jacqueline, who is now my wife, was made much stronger through prayer as we gained insight into the way the other meets God and converses with him. She and I have very different approaches to spirituality, but we were able to get a glimpse of those beautiful differences when we got on our knees, shut out distractions, and opened our hearts to God and to each other. During the time that we spent discerning our relationship together, even after we were engaged, our most intimate moments occurred when we were in prayer and inviting each other into the deepest caverns of our hearts. The intimacy was so strong that we had to be careful not to let it spill over into unintentional physical union prior to marriage, something we were both committed to avoid. There was no doubt that the God who dwells inside each of us, the Holy Spirit, was seeing the life of the other and loving that beauty. Even when the things we were bringing to prayer were scary, sometimes embarrassing, we grew in our desire to be bound in God's love. There have certainly been times in our marriage when things seem to be bigger than either of us can handle on our own or even together, but when we lift our hearts to God through prayer and meditation, the things that matter most in our lives reveal themselves. God's will for us comes alive, and the power to carry it out is found within us.

Making Steps 10 and 11 a regular part of each day allows us to make self-reflection a part of our daily prayer. Maintaining conscious contact with God means regularly checking in to see when we have been close to God and when we have found ourselves distant from him. Some use the guiding principles of a daily inventory in their prayer routine to examine when they were closest to God in a given period (over the past twenty-four hours or during the course of the week) and when they were furthest away. Taking note of these changes can help center us and help us grow in our capacity to be directed by his will.

The Spiritual Exercises of St. Ignatius provide a prayerful blend of daily inventory, or "daily examen" as he called it, and discernment of God's will for us and the power to carry that out. Recovering addicts have plenty to be grateful about, and the importance of maintaining gratitude is outlined in the last chapter of this book. Beginning a prayer routine by giving thanks to the Lord for all that he has done for us on a particular day is a great start to seeing the presence of God in our lives. Acknowledging that presence is a prayerful way of continuing to participate in the grace given us. Furthermore, realizing our limitations and asking God for the ability to see ourselves in an objective way that does not lean too much on either pride or shame is a second point of Ignatius's Spiritual Exercises. This means being able to recognize our sins and the things that get in the way of our usefulness to God and others. Upon seeing these limitations, we quickly amend our behavior so that we may be of maximum service, and ask God for both the courage and strength to carry out what we are called to do.

Jim Harbaugh, S.J., writes and often speaks about the spiritual parallels between the Twelve Steps of recovery and the Spiritual Exercises of St. Ignatius. He describes the Jesuit influence of Alcoholics Anonymous founder Bill Wilson and the moral impact Fr. Ed Dowling, a Jesuit and spiritual mentor to Wilson, had on the development of the Twelve Steps. Harbaugh's book, *A 12-Step Approach to the Spiritual Exercises of St. Ignatius*, takes readers on a retreat-style journey to better understand and prayerfully consider the wonders of Ignatian spirituality. A majority of the book focuses on cultivating a new conscious contact with God by viewing the gospel stories through a creative and personal lens. This is necessary, as he puts it, because, "we may not know very much about this God, this Jesus the Christ. Or we may be struggling with a distorted view of him, just as many newly sober people struggle with a misshapen picture of a monstrous God, left over from their distant childhoods." Harbaugh writes that the best way to come to know God and improve our conscious contact with Christ "is to study his life, death and resurrection." Furthermore, "to know Jesus is to realize that his personal identity is completely intertwined with doing the will of God, whom he called 'Abba,' an affectionate term for 'Father.' As we study Jesus' life, we will simultaneously be pondering how we should best live our lives. In other words, as we 'improve our conscious contact with God'—the God whom Jesus preached—we will concurrently be 'praying only for knowledge of [God's] will for us and the power to carry that out.'"[1]

Coming to know God's will for us can be a great mystery, though as Harbaugh reveals, there are practical ways that we can put our time and attention to use in order to know God. The better we know God, the more likely we are to know what his will for us is.

Contemplating scripture and getting to know Jesus intimately through the stories told in the gospels are essential to developing affection for and understanding Jesus.
I recall the first time I heard the story of the prodigal son,
whom the father ran to and consoled upon his repentant
return home (Lk 15:11–32). It taught me to find mercy in
God and to share that same mercy with others who came
into my life.[2] In another gospel story especially meaningful to me, four faith-filled men carry and lower their
paralytic companion through a crowded house where
Jesus is preaching (Mk 2:1–12). This story has given me
insight into the need for persistence and strength in
bringing ourselves and others to healing through Christ.
It is through the faith of others that our sins can be set
free, and I compared the endurance and action taken by
the four men to the selfless love that I received before
I was able to love myself. That love was given to me
by family, friends, those in Twelve Step communities,
and those in the faithful church community of which
I am blessed to be part. I saw it in the hearts of Chad,
Ross, Aaron, Phil, and Jacob, who were willing to read
scripture with me for the first time as I set a foundation
in my sobriety. I realized that in order to keep the great
gift of faith that was freely given to me, I would have to
be willing to give it back to others who are in need and
may not be able to find it themselves.

Meditation focuses our intellectual and emotional
faculties on a spiritual objective. Having a goal in mind,
even if impossible to achieve, is a way of forging progress through the standard of perfection. Such is getting
to know Jesus. While meditating on the stories told in
both the Old and New Testaments, we can envision ourselves in the place of God's people. When we meditate

with our attention and energy open to God and the Word that dwells among us, we can come to a place where we hear, see, taste, smell, and feel the presence of God through those stories. Many people that have found long runs of sobriety through the grace of God have continued to practice the art of daily meditation and journaling. These daily meditations may come in the form of short readings from addiction recovery resources or from personal dialogue with Jesus. Whatever the source, they are used to guide our prayer and shift our attention from our own wants and worries to a very specific calling that God, through the Holy Spirit, has placed in our hearts.[3]

Many forms of prayer help unite our hearts and intentions with the will of God. Some may choose to integrate well-known Catholic prayers throughout their day. The Lord's Prayer, Hail Mary, traditional before-meal prayers, and other standard forms help lift our hearts to God when we do not have the words ourselves. In other moments, prayer is helpful in sorting out our feelings and actions, revealing where the grace of God is most present in our lives, and strengthening us to avoid occasions where our character defects might get in the way of helping others. This kind of off-the-cuff prayer and meditation can help us in the process of bending our will to meet the will that God has for us. Remember, prayer is not meant to be an effort to bend the will of God to meet what we want or what we think is best for ourselves and others. One of my favorite prayers that shifts my focus away from self-absorbed needs and wants and helps point me to God's will is the Prayer of St. Francis. In recovery circles, this is sometimes known as the Eleventh Step Prayer, and is widely accepted as a standard for how to live selflessly through the desires of God.

> Lord,
> Make me an instrument of your peace.
> Where there is hatred, let me bring love.
> Where there is injury, pardon.
> Where there is doubt, faith.
> Where there is despair, hope.
> Where there is darkness, light.
> Where there is sadness, joy.
> Where there is discord, harmony.
> Where there is error, truth.
> Where there is wrong, the spirit of forgiveness.
> O Divine Master,
> Grant that I may not so much seek
> To be consoled as to console,
> To be understood as to understand,
> To be loved as to love.
> For it is in giving that we receive.
> It is in pardoning that we are pardoned.
> It is in dying that we are born to eternal life.
> Amen.

Through our dedication to living the eleventh step and pursuing God's will for us, we will become channels and instruments of God's love. If we have come to terms with our dark past, we have a responsibility to bring that light into the lives of others. This insight has been fruitful in my relationships with God, others, and myself as I continue to journey through the beautiful landscape of recovery.

Engaging the Sacrament

When asking others how they have overcome the vicious cycle of old behavior patterns and moved toward the freedom offered by Christ's saving grace, I have noticed that there is one response that stands out regularly among those that have found new life in the Catholic Church. A dedication to the Holy Rosary has had a lasting effect on those who have committed themselves to it. As a newly reintroduced Catholic, I was shocked at how many men and women held fast to a relationship with Mary that they maintained through praying the Rosary and meditating on its mysteries.

Maura, who relies on healthy spiritual habits to continue to find healing from an eating addiction and the trauma caused by emotional and physical abuse, shares that the Rosary changed her life. From a young age, she learned the value of routinely praying the Rosary, and the pattern of practicing this devotion regularly was magnified when she came to seek recovery.

> My parents instilled within me from a very young age the power and beauty of the Rosary, so during college I prayed it daily—sometimes out of habit, sometimes from the heart. But desperate situations call for drastic measures, so I decided to pray two Rosaries a day—one in the morning and one at night. The one at night was special (well, all Rosaries are special) and this half hour at night I spent with our Lady was, in my mind, a special meeting with the Queen of Heaven for a petition that I desperately sought wisdom on. I always carried the petition on my heart, and beseeched our Lady to ask her Son to bless me with the grace of forgiveness. I knew she would hear me, as there wasn't an ounce of insincerity in my words, but I didn't know how it would look or feel when the thirty-day "extra Rosary" period was over. I imagined how it would feel or things that would happen, but never

in my wildest dreams did I imagine what actually happened.

It was the eve of the feast of St. Maximilian Kolbe, who is, by the way, the patron saint of Made in His Image [Maura's nonprofit organization].[4] I had finished the extra thirty Rosaries a few days before, and experienced a profound peace within my heart, the peace of forgiveness which produces the grace to see beauty. On that same day, one of the persons who had hurt me sought me out for the first time and asked for my forgiveness with a genuine apology. We cried together as God's grace sliced through the plague of hatred, evil, and anger.

The profound effects and miracles that can come as a result of opening ourselves to God's merciful grace through prayer and meditation have no bounds. Note that the expectations we place on God's will can have detrimental and adverse effects. It is widely shared that our level of serenity is directly inverse to the level of expectation that we set for any given situation. The more we increase our expectations of God, others, and ourselves, the less open we will be to the possibility of what might (or might not) come. I can safely say that the most troubling times I have had in recovery occur when I get too attached to particular outcomes or results. This has been true of my attempts to regain my academic goals, professional expectations that I have set for myself, and the behavior of others that I assume is the best for any given scenario. When my expectations are high, I am tempted into thinking that I must direct the universe, and my relationship with God takes a few steps back. In some cases, I even feel the effects of my forecasts through what can best be referred to as an emotional hangover. Meeting God in prayer and in the Eucharist helps wipe away my need to be the director and wait for the directions of my Creator.

Janice, who overcame the shame of taking a morning-after pill that caused serious bouts of depression, anxiety, and obsessive-compulsive behavior, praises the Rosary for her ascent into a personal relationship with God through Mary. "The Rosary is a tool for me against my running mind and anxiety, because it forces me into a meditative or contemplative state. When I am invited to simply meditate on a scene, it helps guide my prayer. Sometimes when I'm praying, I don't really know what to pray about. I'm just talking, rambling, complaining, or praying for things that I want. When I'm meditating on the mysteries of the Rosary, it helps me to trust God and trust that my prayer is going to be heard. It comes from the heart."

"I pray every day, at various times. Sometimes it's on my way to work, often it includes praying a Rosary each day, which I have been doing for years." This is part of the regular routine central to working Steps 10 and 11. Janice goes on to say, "Writing is a big deal, specifically journal writing, which is a prayer. Sometimes that's journal writing of what's going on in my life, other times it's writing a prayer to God. That's very important to me. I try to do that often. I go to Mass every Sunday, and often during the week. I try to go to confession once a month. I work very well in routines, so I build a routine to my prayer, confession, and taking measures to care for myself. That is part of honoring God, and I do what I can to be healthy: for me that is going to counseling, exercising, journaling, meeting with other people."

A well-known Catholic spiritual writer and president of the Oblate School of Theology, Ronald Rolheiser writes about the manifold characteristics of the Eucharist in his book *Our One Great Act of Fidelity: Waiting for Christ in the Eucharist*. Describing the unifying power of the Eucharist, he explains the importance of this sacrament to personal prayer and devotion. "The Eucharist is such a prayer of helplessness, a prayer for God to give us a unity we cannot give to ourselves. . . . It is not incidental that Jesus instituted it in the hour of his most intense loneliness, when he realized that all the words he had spoken hadn't been enough and that he had no more words to give. When he felt most helpless, he gave us the prayer of helplessness, the Eucharist." Recognizing generational trends that keep us from hearing God in the silence of our lives and the constant demand that we ought to be rulers of our own domain, Rolheiser recaps the basic principles of Twelve Step recovery as he articulates our need to seek the Eucharist to overcome our wounds. "We must turn our helplessness into a Quaker silence, a Eucharistic prayer that asks God to come and do for us what we cannot do for ourselves: create community. We must go to Eucharist for this reason."[5]

Like me, Janice found strength through the church community centered on celebrating the beauty of the Eucharist. "Mass and the Eucharist is a regular anchor for me," she explains. "I try to go to adoration at least once a week as well. The beautiful thing about the Eucharist is that, because I am so often in my head and I like to think that I can figure things out, there is no thinking involved. It's beautiful, because with the Eucharist you can come to the table and receive, and you don't just think about it. It is just God present and you receive, or adore while in adoration, and that helps quiet my mind with a simplicity that is very important to the faith life.

Sometimes I struggle finding that simplicity, and the Eucharist helps me with that."

When we celebrate Mass, a transformation takes place that becomes the central focus and summit of our gathering. It is the transformation, or *transubstantiation*, that occurs when the bread and wine become Christ. At this moment, we have the opportunity to offer ourselves to be transformed into Christ, and our partaking in the Body and Blood of Christ does just that. This completes our conscious contact with God as we understand him, and when brought to the banquet in a prayerful and reflective light, Step 11 is united with the sacred mystery of the Eucharist. When we make ourselves truly present in prayer and meditation, we experience moments when we can feel the loving embrace of God the Father. He unites us to himself to share his love with us. In the same way, we have the chance to receive the body of his Son, Jesus Christ, whose great gift to us was the Eucharist, instituted at the Last Supper and handed down from generation to generation.

Rolheiser continues his reflection on the sacrifice that Christ made for us in the Eucharist. "We participate in Jesus' sacrifice for us when we, like him, let ourselves be broken down, when we, like him, become selfless. The Eucharist, as sacrifice, invites us to become like the kernels of wheat that make up the bread and the clusters of grapes that make up the wine, broken down and crushed so that we can become part of the communal loaf and single cup."[6] Those in recovery know all about being broken down. We lived through the process, fighting and rationalizing that we had things under control. After enough brokenness and pain, we are now invited to take part in something greater than ourselves. We are invited into a fellowship that joins in unity to provide recovery for all, the old and the new. Through working the steps and seeing how the lives of others have unfolded, we learn that the way of selflessness is the better option, and we are given to gradually make that a part of our daily lives. Being a part of the whole, we are now tasked with one more mission—a mission that will be our life's work as long as we remain sober.

"What is supposed to happen at the Eucharist," Rolheiser continues, "is that we, the congregation, by sacrificing the things that divide us, should become the body and blood of Christ. More so than the bread and wine, we, the people, are meant to be changed, to be transubstantiated. The Eucharist, as sacrifice, asks us to become the bread of brokenness and the chalice of vulnerability."[7] While being vulnerable and open with our inherent brokenness, we are now sent out. We are called to give back and to share the Good News with as many people as we can while practicing these principles in all our affairs. Just as in the proclamation that we hear at the conclusion of Mass after becoming united with the Body of Christ, we are called to bring the fruits of the Eucharist to the world: "Go in peace to love and serve the Lord."

✝

Let Us Pray

Lord,
I enter into prayer with you
knowing it is not perfect collection of words
that you seek, but a contrite and loving heart
yearning for union with you.

As my prayer life develops,
let me remember that all I have is gift,
including my faith life
and the propensity to seek you
through prayer and the sacraments.
Thank you for your ultimate sacrifice,
so that I may know you intimately and personally
here on earth while anticipating perfect union
with you in heaven.
Amen.

Going Further

1. What is your prayer life like?
2. In what ways have you personally experienced God through the Eucharist?
3. How can you enrich and enlarge your conscious contact with God through both prayer and participation in the Sacrament of the Eucharist?
4. Seek another individual that has a God-conscious attitude toward life and ask him or her how they pray. Humbly seek ways to improve your conscious contact with God.
5. Set aside time to be silent and pray each day. This may begin with just five minutes a day, but choose a time that you can go back to regularly. After you have established a routine, expand the amount of time that you are committing to prayer on a daily basis.

CONFIRMATION

12.

AWAKENING
AND CALL

I met John during my first week of recovery. He was at a few Twelve Step meetings that I attended, and suggested one day that we get a cup of coffee together and get to know each other a little bit. This kind of friendly invitation from mostly complete strangers was, I began to notice, a regular way that these people conducted themselves, offering their time to walk alongside those that were new to the program. We sat down together at a coffee shop a day or two later, and John began to share some of his story with me. I couldn't help but notice his raspy voice as he talked, as well as how vulnerable he made himself on that first meeting together. He was very confident in himself, even as he dug into his dark past. At the time, this was all new to me and made me wonder how he and so many others were able to hold their heads high while revealing many of the things that I was completely ashamed of.

There was a moment in John's past when he was in a place of such great darkness and loneliness that his best idea was to take his own life. He took the actions to make it happen. He bought a gun, got the ammunition, and was ready for the time to come. With the cold metal of the gun entering his mouth, he was prepared to put an end to his horror. Then, suddenly, a thought came to him: "What if there actually is a God?" Not certain whatsoever, but filled with enough doubt to want to live another day, he put the gun down. He was too much of a coward to pull the trigger. Or, perhaps, he was blessed with just enough faith—faith the size of a mustard seed—to continue his journey.

John was born and raised in Chicago. After attending an all-boys high school and a Catholic university in Green Bay, Wisconsin, he joined the Navy and became a pilot. It takes a special kind of man to fly jets, and John did just that. He flew an F-4 Phantom, a two-seat, twin-engine supersonic jet, through two tours during the Vietnam War. He recalls flying about 230 missions during his time in the Navy. It was around this time that the allure of alcohol became too great, and John transitioned from using alcohol to deal with pain and celebrate victories to drinking through every endeavor in his life.

A series of consequences unfolded that ultimately took his will to live—that is, until God intervened that day he put the gun in his mouth. Finding a life of sobriety was not easy for him. In fact, it would be the hardest thing that he ever attempted. After a few failed tries, he committed himself to getting involved in a fellowship and working the Twelve Steps as outlined by his sponsor. He soon began noticing the fruits of his efforts and God's grace unfold in his life. He tells me:

> First and most important, I worked through the
> steps with a good sponsor. I had to do it a couple

of times, back to back, to work through the obvious
things, and to get rid of the big chunks of wreckage
from my past. Over the years, I've gone through
them again and again, especially when I've caught
myself feeling a little lost. They've never failed to
get me back on track. After a few years, my life
started getting better, a lot better, but that presented
a whole new set of challenges. That's when I learned
the steps aren't just about dealing with your past;
the steps provide the tools to deal with the present
in such a way that you can build a great future.

John began sponsoring a number of other men. He
married his wife, Mona, and has remained committed to
her. Their relationship together is founded on the principles of the Twelve Steps, as is the rest of John's life.
Beyond that, over the years, he has found the steps to
be the perfect blueprint to follow in every situation he
has encountered. The Twelve Steps were useful when he
went back to school, bringing him to admit that he was
powerless over his procrastination, his fear, his teachers,
and his required courses. He came to believe he could be
restored to a new way of looking at those things. "When
I got my first job after graduation," he explains, "I used
the steps to guide my work habits and to guide my relationships with my coworkers. When I got promoted to
management, I used the steps as my business plan. With
the steps to guide me, I was promoted time after time,
and had a very successful career. I always used to tell
Mona on payday that I felt like the check was made out
to the wrong guy."

While describing John, I have to give you a bit of
insight into his humility and the humor that he has carried with him throughout his time in recovery. Reflecting

on how God's guidance has taken him to heights he
never dreamed, he recalls what life used to be like before
he got sober. "I was just as smart, just as talented, and
even more cute than I am now. However, I parlayed
those advantages into two divorces, unemployability,
homelessness, and fantasies of suicide. Not bad, huh?
The only difference between the broken, pitiful little
guy that showed up here and the guy who's received so
many wonderful gifts over the last thirty-one years is the
fellowship I found, the Twelve Steps, and the support
and examples of many great men."

John's successful career came in the health care field,
first as a nurse and then as part of the leadership team
that managed the direction of several hospitals. I have
witnessed some of his former employees share their feelings about him, and it is a treasure to see how beloved
he is by those who were under his direction. Many of
those people have come forward to care for John and
show their support in light of some recent difficulties.

When I met John, he was twenty-four years sober
and a new challenge was coming his way. His hoarse
voice, it was soon determined, was a symptom of a
life-altering disease that he has been living with over the
past five or six years. John was diagnosed with amyo-
trophic lateral sclerosis (ALS), sometimes known as Lou
Gehrig's disease. It started taking his physical abilities
away from him, beginning in his throat and muting his
voice. ALS then worked its way through the rest of his
body, handicapping him and limiting him to a wheel-
chair. No longer could he play golf with his buddies,
walk his dog, or stay active with the host of friends that
were a close part of his life. This new life that was now
being taken from him, by the way, was a far cry from the

lonely despair of a man who once sat with a gun in his mouth wishing for the courage to end it all.

Since his voice is gone, John now communicates with an iPad and an app that speaks the words he types in a monotone voice. That is now the voice that I know of as John. Thanks to limited use of his right hand, he can still type at a very slow rate.

All of the sad facets of John's condition are adequate reasons to be consumed by anguish, fear, and self-pity. But John would not want this to be the point of emphasis made. Instead, his wish would be to frame his situation by the fullness of grace that God has given him to peacefully accept all that has taken place in his life. That started with a spiritual awakening and has been maintained by practicing these principles in all of his affairs. In fact, *grateful* is a term I hear him use much more often than would ever be expected or seem to be warranted for someone in John's place.

> As far as the impact ALS has had on me, obviously it's physically devastating, so I don't want to dwell on that. There are many positives that have come to me from this. Although I would never volunteer for it, if I let myself accept this is happening to me, I can appreciate the deep inner journey that is opening up to me if I choose to follow the path. None of this is original, but it has become real for me over the last several years. First, I've come to know that I am not my body. I never would have seen that if not for ALS. As you can see, my body is becoming totally useless. Yet I, whatever "I" am, am still in here. I am still the same guy I always have been. I am genuinely happy the great majority of the time.

Step 12 suggests that having had a spiritual awakening as a result of working the steps, we try to carry this message to others with a similar condition, and to practice these principles in all our affairs. By working the Twelve Steps on a daily basis, John was receiving gifts from God that he would use in some of his most difficult and trying times. This grace keeps him centered and has allowed him to live the last years of his life with dignity. He is beginning to have other realizations. He explains that there are times when he is overcome with sadness and starts feeling sorry for himself. "Self-pity can be intoxicating," he types. He is coming to know his Higher Power in a deeper and more profound way than he did prior to his ALS diagnosis, having to put his trust in the Source that has supported him throughout the early days of recovery and through the trial that he currently finds himself in. "The gift that ALS has given me is that, on a practical level, I am experiencing my Higher Power on a tangible, personal level."

It is difficult to see John in the state he is in now. Selfishly, I struggle with it, knowing that there are no more rounds of golf together in our future and less wit and wisdom from long conversations that are not aided by a machine. He has been a deep source of comfort for me, beginning with that first exchange over coffee when I was timid to share the fullness of my struggle. He led the way that day by being vulnerable himself, and continues to be vulnerable while showing me the way of faith. Others that have given themselves selflessly, including John's wife Mona and his best friend Ron, have been a great example of giving back to John the fruits of what he has given them.

He may not live much longer here on earth, but the impact that John has had on me and others will live forever. This includes Mona, his family, the men and women whom he has guided through recovery (and who have since gone on to guide, or sponsor, others), the hundreds, if not thousands, of people who have worked under his leadership (and received the wisdom of the Twelve Steps without even realizing it), and the people whose lives will be made better and more peaceful because John helped their loved one stay sober. John's legacy, through the call and strength of God, will live on and impact generations to come.

One of the greatest gifts that I have received with sobriety is found in relationships. As it was said to me, "relationships are going to be the most important aspect of your recovery." This truth develops in a number of different ways. Repaired relationships have come back to life, and new relationships have formed. A beautiful thing happens when an individual fed up with the damage being caused by his lifestyle of addiction reaches out for help. This is where Step 12 and Step 1 unite. My dark past has become one of my greatest assets, helping me remain in the grace that accompanies a spiritual awakening and giving me the ability to relate to others swimming in darkness.

Witnessing new life take root in a man or woman who was once hopeless is a marvelous thing. It is one of many reasons I keep coming back to recovery fellowship, so that I can relive the miracle that has taken place in my own life and so that I may be of service to others who might benefit from me sharing my experience, strength, and hope. While God has blessed me with some platforms to reach people on a wider scale, such as this book that you hold in your hands, nothing tops the one-on-one interaction with another who shares similar experiences with alcoholism, drug addiction, or other addictive behaviors. Few things bring me back to gratitude or bring more meaning to my life than a phone call, text message, or email from someone looking to curb their addiction. One addict helping another is the foundation on which Twelve Step recovery was formed. Christ's kingdom here on earth was spread in the same way. Through our encounters with others, we gain unique insight and come to encounter Jesus Christ.

A gift is not truly a gift unless it can be given away, and those that I have written about in previous chapters have done just that. Maura Preszler, who spoke to me about her difficulty in overcoming eating disorders and abuse, once feared being alone. When I interviewed her, she was holding her four-month-old son, Pio, and had recently celebrated her one-year anniversary with her husband, Michael. "I got married, although I never thought that would happen. My husband has helped me overcome a lot, and I never thought I would be able to take those steps in a relationship and show the required amount of vulnerability. I am so thankful to God that he has blessed me with all the things that I have today, which I only have because of my healing. I never would have been able to be in a healthy relationship, get married, or give birth to a baby," she exclaimed to me with a big smile on her face. Pio had an equally large grin as she bounced him on her lap, unable to hold in her gratitude.

Maura has made a profound impact on other women who struggle with identity, abuse, eating disorders, and the struggles of womanhood. Her nonprofit organization, Made in His Image, was created in 2011 and reaches nearly 50,000 individuals while restoring strength to those that are suffering. "I called it Made in His Image because my recovery was, and is, such an important part of discovering my identity as a daughter of God. I really want to help other women who struggle the way that I have, and there are so many of them. I really believe that we can't see who we are created to be if we do not know what that is. I think a lot of people don't know what they were called for, and that saddens me." The mission of Made in His Image is to begin a dialogue, a discussion, in a safe and compassionate setting, to foster hope and healing, and to empower women to turn from victim to survivor. Ultimately, the vision is to provide holistic medical treatment and healing for women suffering from eating disorders and physical and/or sexual abuse, which entails educating all women on the nature and dignity of the human person, created in the image and likeness of God. Maura also gives talks throughout the country, where she shares her story and speaks on topics that encourage healing.

Janice's life has turned from the fabric of fear, loneliness, and depression to one where she uses her skills and service to help others. Meeting regularly with those who are interested in growing in their faith and having a life rooted in the Good News, she sets aside several hours a week to visit one-on-one with those she can help. Her service to others is an imperative and helps her stay on the path of spiritual freedom and emotional and mental health. "I try to give my time to meet with other people from a ministry standpoint, which includes staying active to give back what I have received. I have to give back; otherwise, even if I don't sin, my thoughts will become very negative and self-absorbed, which is very difficult for me to battle with," she explains. She is active in her church parish and uses her skills as a writer to share the faith with others.

Ever since Thomas worked through the six-month alcohol and drug rehabilitation treatment that his father helped him get into, he has used the Twelve Steps to guide his life. Working through the steps multiple times has revealed a variety of issues that needed attention throughout his twenty-two years of sobriety. Insights into problems with anger have helped him mellow his demeanor, and other reflections have helped him understand the failure of previous long-term romantic relationships. This work has helped him develop into a man that loves God, serves his family, and helps others. I have been privileged to experience the direct fruit of that service as Thomas has been my sponsor since I was about eight months sober. He has walked me through a lot of difficult moments while I worked through the steps and dealt with disappointments. He was there to celebrate with my wife and me as we took our marriage vows. In fact, he was a driving force in helping me prepare myself to be a man that was able to be in a committed relationship. He has shown me what sacrifice for the sake of others who are suffering is all about, as he is readily available to help men get sober and work with them through the Twelve Steps of recovery.

Since finding freedom, faith, and fellowship in Twelve Step recovery and the Catholic Church, many opportunities have presented themselves to me. It's amazing what can happen when a few twenty-four hours of sobriety are strung together. Relationships with those I love and care about have a new richness to them, especially as we mend our past to create a brighter future. After struggling through the process of getting accepted into a four-year university, I was given a chance by a reputable Christian university in San Diego. In May 2017 I received my bachelors degree with my parents and wife there to support me. It was a beautiful day that held all the emotion of more than a decade of extreme highs and lows.

God made it pretty clear that he had plans for me to use my experience for the benefit of others. In response to some general directions he had given me through prayer and circumstances unfolding in my life, Catholic in Recovery was formed. It is a nonprofit Catholic ministry that serves communities by equipping parishes and individuals with tools to minister to those struggling with addictions and unhealthy attachments.[1] In a brief period of time, we have been able to accompany those already in addiction recovery into full communion with the Catholic Church while also aiding individuals already active in the Church who are suffering from a variety of addictions. Witnessing God's miracles work in the lives of others reminds me of the beautiful portrait—God's masterpiece—that my friend Dorothy used to describe to me. When I step back to appreciate the whole thing, I see God still placing brushstrokes while asking me to remain in him.

Engaging the Sacrament

The Church explains that the reception of the Sacrament of Confirmation is required to complete baptismal grace. The Spirit and the gifts we receive in Baptism reach their fulfillment only if we go into the world and spread the seeds of faith, in the same way that the work we do when we begin the Twelve Steps—with all of our bro-kenness and powerlessness—is not complete until we are prepared to touch the souls of those who are in the same place we once were. Confirmation gives us special grace and strengthens associated gifts of the Holy Spirit, so that we may confess our faith through our actions and our words. Living fully in the truth that the confirmed is an anointed daughter or son of Christ is bound to attract others who are seeking a life of fulfillment.

Confirmation continues the succession of the faith-ful that have walked the earth since the days of Christ. It ensures that our faith remains for generations to come. A beautiful connection to the ancient Church is signified by the laying on of hands, an outward sign of a movement that began with the apostles. In a similar way, when one alcoholic works with another or when one recover-ing gambling addict shares his hope with another that is seeking healing, they are continuing the movement that started Twelve Step recovery in the 1930s. In the process, each is strengthened and gets to know God in a new way through the other. There is a set of spiritual gifts, often referred to as the gifts of the Holy Spirit, that are passed on through the Sacrament of Confirmation. These gifts, much like the fruits of the Twelve Steps, are offered for the sake of something greater. Confirmation occurs for the sake of the Church. We are strengthened for an objective that is beyond our individual ability and to participate in a greater cause, perhaps *the* greatest cause—to grow the mission of Christ through the work of the Church and share the Good News of his salvation.

The gifts of the Holy Spirit are wisdom, knowledge, understanding, fortitude, counsel, piety, and fear of the Lord. Wisdom, knowledge, and understanding offer us

a deep spiritual vision and allow us to see the world
from the standpoint of God. This is part of the interior
reformation that continues to take place as we learn the
beauty of living selflessly and with deeper meaning
through recovery. These gifts aim to shed self-seeking
interests so that, properly armed with the facts about
ourselves and equipped with the full armor of God, we
can use our newly found trust in the Lord for his divine
mission. It does not take gray-haired wisdom to make
this possible. Rather, understanding how our experience
can benefit others and propel us to properly serve the
Lord allows any of us, at any age and with any level of
education, to help others.

Fortitude, or courage, shapes our resolve to battle
temptation and other forces that may prowl among us
hoping to get us off our path. God offers gifts of courage to overcome these distractions and the fortitude to
defend the faith in a prudent way. A prayer that is popular among addicts in recovery is the Serenity Prayer,
which is said together at many Twelve Step meetings.
While encompassing the necessary attitude and reliance
upon God to give us the grace to get through our day,
this prayer also summons the strength to seek gifts and
virtues that bring us to peace. The longer version of the
Serenity Prayer is less well known, but relates to the
topic of fortitude:

> God, grant me the serenity
> To accept the things I cannot change,
> Courage to change the things I can,
> And Wisdom to know the difference.
> Living one day at a time,
> Enjoying one moment at a time,
> Accepting hardship as the pathway to peace.

Taking, as He did, this sinful world as it is,
not as I would have it.
Trusting that He will make all things right
if I surrender to His will.
That I may be reasonably happy in this life,
And supremely happy with Him forever in the next.

Counsel, piety, and fear of the Lord are gifts that instill within us a deep sense of our duty as confirmed Catholics. That means doing what has been laid out in front of us. At this stage in our progress, that means consistently completing Steps 10 and 11 so that we may maintain our connection with God and conduct our relationships with integrity. Our duty comes from the service imperative to give back what we have been freely given. I believe that I will never be able to give back all that I have received through my recovery, yet I feel a sense of responsibility to actively contribute to the causes that gave me new life.

As a result of a spiritual awakening, which may come quicker to some than to others, we have been given a new way of life. God consciousness—formed by surrendering our lives to a God that we may not completely understand, becoming honest with our shortcomings and fears, seeking the power of God to remove our defects of character, making reparation for the wrongs we have done to others, and continuing to foster our conscious contact with God—will be the new lens through which we see the world. In this view, God comes first. This is the gift known as fear of the Lord. Emmet Fox, a New Thought spiritual leader of the early twentieth century, puts it best: "Sooner or later you will have to put God first in your life. God must become the only thing that really matters. It need not be, and better not be, the only thing in your life, but it must be the first thing. When that happens your life becomes simple, richer, and infinitely more worthwhile."[2]

Organizing our lives around God, we draw interest as we bear witness to a life of firm dedication. Especially today, when structuring our lives around a sense of duty to God and others is radically different from how our culture suggests we live, we spark apostolic interest. This interest increases if we are beginning to live our lives in a vastly different way than how we did before. Confirmation is a sacrament of evangelization. As one of the guiding traditions of Twelve Step recovery proclaims, we begin living our lives, and evangelical efforts, based on attraction rather than promotion. When a life is lived in the Spirit, those who seek something greater and more worthwhile tend to be attracted to that life. That was my experience with Brock as he guided me through the early stages of life in the Catholic Church. That is now our duty as those who have been blessed with a spiritual awakening and have received the Sacrament of Confirmation. We are sent on a mission. Confirmation makes us significant, yet humble, participants in salvation, as initiated by the sacrifice of Christ. We are now coheirs to that sacrifice.

One man or woman can change the world. The Spirit will work through you in extraordinary ways and has great plans to use your life to spread the faith to others. Do not be afraid. Do not let discouragement bring you down. Know that all of your experiences, even the darkest of moments, can be useful to further the kingdom of God. The stories told here along with the millions of untold tales around the world bear witness to this truth. Do not underestimate the kind of impact that your life will have on those you touch.

Although the day of my Confirmation as a young seventeen-year-old was quickly followed by the day of my first drink, the gifts that were planted within me and the grace made available to me through the sacrament were making their mark. The first drink led me down a slide of difficult times, but I believe that the hidden grace that came from Confirmation, which completed my baptismal plunge into the Christian life, strengthened me when I was ready to surrender. God made that possible. He never stopped pursuing me, and he will never stop pursuing you.

†

Let Us Pray

Lord,
Thank you for never giving up your pursuit of me.
Having had a spiritual awakening,
I wish to let go of the things I think I know
and, instead, hold tightly
to the love that you have for me
and to the mission
that you have sent me forth to do.
Every step of my recovery journey
has been paved by you,
and you have crafted me beautifully.
Please allow me to see the world
through your lenses
so that I may be of maximum service to you
and to those around me.
May I do for others what your love has done for
me.

In all things, give me a heart that seeks the weary,
the lonely, and the hopeless
so that, one day, we may all be united
in your heavenly kingdom.
Amen.

Going Further

1. How has God provided a spiritual awakening in your life? Has it been a gradual process or one that has developed quickly?
2. Who are the people in your life that have been there to witness to God's love and the saving mercy of our Divine Physician?
3. In what areas of your life can you apply the principles of Twelve Step recovery?
4. Who in your life may need help through a difficult moment, addiction, or unhealthy attachment?
5. Are you living your life with greater meaning and purpose, serving the Lord so that his love shines through you?
6. How do you make yourself available to those who may rely upon your help and gain hope from your experience? Are you willing to be vulnerable with them and humbly detail the way God has reformed your life.

NOTES

Introduction

1. I refer here to the Twelve Steps of Alcoholics Anonymous, as put forth in the book *Alcoholics Anonymous: The Story of How Many Thousands of Men and Women Have Recovered from Alcoholism*, 4th ed. (New York: Alcoholics Anonymous World Services, 2001). Commonly known as "The Big Book," this is the primary addiction literature referred to in this book. Other Twelve Step groups have been adapted to fit specific addictions, mostly through the same Twelve Steps proposed by Alcoholics Anonymous.

Powerless and Unmanageable

1. *Catechism of the Catholic Church* (Vatican City: Libreria Editrice Vaticana, 1994), 1792.

2. Order of Mass, 4, *The Roman Missal*, 3rd ed. (Washington, DC: US Conference of Catholic Bishops, 2011).

Come to Believe

1. Ernest Kurtz and Katherine Ketcham have written one of the best books on addiction recovery through the wisdom of the Twelve Steps: *The Spirituality of Imperfection: Storytelling and the Search for Meaning* (New York: Bantam Books, 1992).

Turning Our Will Over to God

1. For more information on the work that Dr. Kleponis does to help those struggling with pornography addiction, visit www.integrityrestored.com. Another great Catholic website that offers resources for men and women looking to find freedom from pornography is www.theporneffect. com.

2. For further insight into the effect that shame plays in our lives, I suggest reading John Bradshaw, *Healing the Shame That Binds You* (Deerfield Beach, FL: Health Communications, 1988).

Admitting Our Wrongs

1. An excellent book that tells the story of those who have found freedom from pornography addiction is Matt Fradd, *Delivered: True Stories of Men and Women Who Turned from Porn to Purity* (San Diego: Catholic Answers Press, 2013).

2. There are a variety of accountability software programs available to monitor and block unwanted websites. One that I have found particularly helpful in monitoring pornography use is Covenant Eyes. For more information, visit www.covenanteyes.com.

Removing Defects

1. For more information on sexual chastity, Jason Evert's Chastity Project (www.chastityproject.com) has blogs, books, and media focused on the topic. For chastity-related resources specifically designed for women, Crystalina Evert's ministry and website, Women Made New (www.womenmadenew.com), encourages women in need of personal healing. For resources on emotional chastity, visit www.emotionalvirtue.com.

A Humble Request

1. A book that takes a focused look at the fruits of Steps 6 and 7 is Bill P., Todd W., and Sara S., *Drop the Rock: Removing Character Defects*, 2nd ed. (Center City, MN: Hazelden, 2005).

2. *Catechism of the Catholic Church*, 1435.

Continued Personal Inventory

1. *Catechism of the Catholic Church*, 1360.

2. Ibid., 1436.

Conscious Contact with God

1. Jim Harbaugh, S.J., *A 12-Step Approach to the Spiritual Exercises of St. Ignatius* (Franklin, WI: Sheed & Ward, 1997), 48.

2. My understanding of the wisdom behind the biblical parable of the prodigal son was enhanced by reading Henri Nouwen's book *The Return of the Prodigal Son: A Story of Homecoming* (1992). It captures the story from all angles and is a book about mercy that I strongly recommend.

3. Some suggestions for daily meditations include:

- *Jesus Calling: Enjoying Peace in His Presence*, by Sarah Young.
- *Twenty-Four Hours a Day* (Anonymous)—Dorothy strongly suggested I read this every day.
- *My Daily Bread: A Summary of the Spiritual Life*, by Anthony J. Paone, S.J.

4. For more information on Maura Preszler's nonprofit organization, Made in His Image, visit www.madeinhisimage.org.

5. Ronald Rolheiser, O.M.I., *Our One Great Act of Fidelity: Waiting for Christ in the Eucharist* (New York: Image, 2011), 40.

6. Ibid., 60.

7. Ibid.

Awakening and Call

1. For more information on Catholic in Recovery, visit www.catholicinrecovery.com.

2. The writings of Dr. Emmet Fox center around a universal need to understand who God is in relation to our own lives. The vocabulary he uses to describe this relationship with God is consistent with the language of Twelve Step recovery. A few suggested readings of his include: *The Sermon on the Mount, Power through Constructive Thinking*, and *Find and Use Your Inner Power*.

Scott Weeman is the founder and executive director of Catholic in Recovery, a nonprofit organization that seeks to help those suffering with addictions.

Weeman has appeared on EWTN's *The Journey Home*, as well as *Christopher Closeup*, *Catholic Answers*, and *The Catholic Hipster Podcast*. His work has been featured on *Aleteia* and *Patheos*. He earned his bachelor's degree in organizational management in 2017 from Point Loma Nazarene University where he is a graduate student in clinical counseling.

He lives in San Diego, California, with his wife, Jacqueline.

AVE
AVE MARIA PRESS

Founded in 1865, Ave Maria Press,
a ministry of the Congregation of
Holy Cross, is a Catholic publishing
company that serves the spiritual and
formative needs of the Church and its
schools, institutions, and ministers;
Christian individuals and families; and
others seeking spiritual nourishment.

For a complete listing of titles from

Ave Maria Press

Sorin Books

Forest of Peace

Christian Classics

visit www.avemariapress.com

AVE MARIA PRESS
Notre Dame, IN
A Ministry of the United States Province of Holy Cross